D1104746

# FACTS ABOUT
# FINLAND

Otava Publishing Company Limited
Helsinki

© Kustannusosakeyhtiö Otava
Otava Publishing Company Ltd., 1991, 1993, 1994

Published by Otava Publishing Company Ltd.
Uudenmaankatu 8–12, SF-00120 Helsinki, Finland

Text editing  by Matti Eskola
Lay-out by Sinikka Lindfors
Translated by Michael Wynne-Ellis

3rd edition

Printed in Finland by Otava Printing Works
Keuruu 1994

ISBN 951-1-13555-4

# CONTENTS

**THE LAND AND THE PEOPLE 5**
Topography 6
Coasts and archipelagos 6
Inland waters 6
Climate 8
Flora and fauna 8
Conservation of nature and the environment 11
Origin of the Finns 11
Population growth 12
Settlement 13
**A TRAVELLER'S FINLAND 16**
Finnish cuisine 22
**Tourist areas 27**
South-west Finland 27
The lake district 29
Bothnia 29
East Finland 31
Lapland 31
The rights and duties of tourists 32
Importance of the tourist industry 32
Tourist authorities and organisations 33
**THE STATE 34**
Constitution and form of government 34
The President of the Republic 34
The Council of State and the administration 36
Political parties 38
Local government 39
The judiciary 41
**HISTORY 42**
Prehistory 42
The Swedish period (c. 1200–1809) 42
The autonomous Grand Duchy of Finland (1809–1917) 45
Independent Finland (1917 onwards) 49
**FOREIGN POLICY 56**
Finland and the other Nordic nations 57
Finland and the Soviet Union 57
Relations with other countries 59
Finland and the United Nations 61
**SECURITY AND DEFENCE POLICY 64**
**THE ECONOMY 68**
Foreign trade 70
Agriculture and forestry 73
Industry 76
Construction 78
Domestic trade 78
Transport and communications 79
Banking and insurance 80
The public sector 82
Consumption and the standard of living 84
Balancing the national economy 84
**SOCIAL SECURITY 85**
Health insurance 85
Pension insurance 86
Unemployment assistance 86
Accident insurance 87
Family allowances 87
Care of the elderly 88
**Health care 88**
Health centres 88
Hospitals 90
Patients 91
Environmental health 91
Housing policy 91
Labour policy 92
**THE CHURCH 94**
**SCHOOLS AND EDUCATION 99**
Pre-school education 99
Comprehensive schools 100
Senior secondary education 102
Higher education 105
Research 109
Adult education 110
**CULTURE 113**
Folk traditions and festivals 113
Traditional handicrafts 117
Sami culture 118
Literature 118
Libraries 125
Music 126
Dance 133
Design 135
Theatre 137
Cinema 139
Architecture 141
Painting 144
Sculpture 149
**RADIO, TELEVISION AND THE PRESS 153**
Radio and the history of broadcasting 153
Television 154
The press 156
**SPORT 158**
The most popular sports 158
Great Finnish victories 158
The importance of sport in Finland 163
**THE FINNISH LIFESTYLE 164**
**WHO'S WHO IN FINLAND 173**
**SELECTED BIBLIOGRAPHY 189**

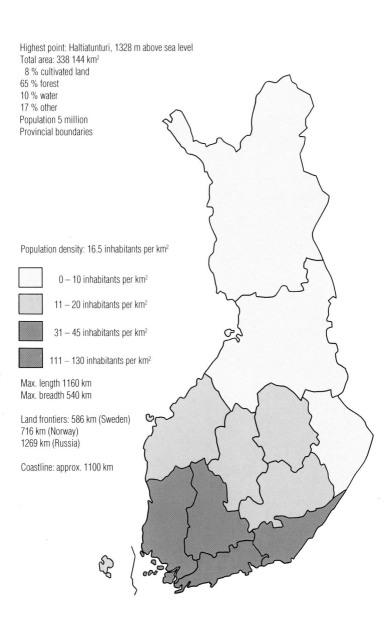

Highest point: Haltiatunturi, 1328 m above sea level
Total area: 338 144 km$^2$
  8 % cultivated land
65 % forest
10 % water
17 % other
Population 5 million
Provincial boundaries

Population density: 16.5 inhabitants per km$^2$

    0 – 10 inhabitants per km$^2$

  11 – 20 inhabitants per km$^2$

  31 – 45 inhabitants per km$^2$

111 – 130 inhabitants per km$^2$

Max. length 1160 km
Max. breadth 540 km

Land frontiers: 586 km (Sweden)
716 km (Norway)
1269 km (Russia)

Coastline: approx. 1100 km

**Population density map**

# THE LAND AND THE PEOPLE

With a total area of 338 145 km$^2$, Finland is the seventh largest country in Europe. The longest distance from south to north is 1160 km and the greatest width 540 km. Its total frontier is 3600 km in length, 2571 km are land borders; 586 km with Sweden, 716 km with Norway, and 1269 km with Russia. The coastline is about 1100 km long. Approximately 70 % of the land surface is forest, 15 % cultivated land, settlement or roads and 15 % wasteland, such as swamps, artic fells and sand.

The population of Finland in 1992 reached the 5 million mark, which makes it one of the smallest countries in Europe. Among the Nordic countries, only Norway and Iceland are smaller. The average population density is 16.5 inhabitants/km$^2$, which varies from 130 in the industrialised south to between 2 and 3 in the sparsely populated regions of the north.

Finland may be classified as a post-industrial nation, and in 1990 an estimated 9 % of the population derived its livelihood from agriculture, 33 % from industry, and 58 % from services.

**Finland is the most northerly country in the world: one quarter of its total area lies north of the Arctic Circle. By air from Finland it is 6600 km to New York, 7800 km to Tokyo and 9600 km to Johannesburg.**

## TOPOGRAPHY

Part of the Finnish bedrock is among the oldest in the world, and is covered with moraine. The present relief of the country was fashioned during the last Ice Age. The continental glacier gouged the lake basins that run north-west to south-east, and when it ceased it left on its edges the Salpausselkä ridges that run east north-east to west north-west. The fast-flowing currents from the melting glaciers created the numerous ridges, which run in the same direction as the lake basins. The most famous of these ridges or eskers is the lake-surrounded Punkaharju near Savonlinna. Another reminder of the continental glacier is the fact that the land mass is still rising: along the Gulf of Finland the land rises 30 cm every hundred years, and on the Gulf of Bothnia by as much as 90 cm. The land mass thus increases by about 7 $km^2$ annually.

Most of Finland is low-lying plain. There are lowlands and plains along the Gulf of Bothnia and to a certain extent in the coastal areas along the Gulf of Finland, where the land begins to rise to form mounds and hills broken by lakes and waterways. The average height above sea level is 152 m. The only true highland area is in Enontekiö, Lapland, where Finland's highest points are: Halti (1328 m) and Saana (1029 m).

## COASTS AND ARCHIPELAGOS

To the south and west, Finland is bounded by the shallow Baltic Sea, the world's largest basin of brackish water, the Gulf of Finland and the Gulf of Bothnia. The fragmented south-western coastline continues into Saaristo-meri, with over 17 000 islands and skerries. As the land is continuously rising, new skerries keep emerging from the sea. To the west of Saaristomeri are the extensive Åland Islands. If an island is classified as a land mass of over 100 $m^2$ surrounded by water, then there are some 81 000 of them within Finnish territorial waters.

## INLAND WATERS

Relative to its size, Finland has more lakes than any other country. There are 187 888 lakes over 5 acres in size, and 22 over 200 $km^2$ in area, of which 2 are artificial reservoirs. The fourth largest lake in Europe, the 4 400 $km^2$ Lake Saimaa, forms a mosaic of water, rocks, forests and fields in the south-east of the country. Other lakes over 1000 $km^2$ in size are Päijänne and Inari. The average depth of lakes is 7 m and the deepest ever measured is 95 m. The overall volume of lake water is only slightly more than the average annual rainfall. In many places it is still possible for local residents and summer house owners to drink from the clean, clear lakes. There are over 98 000 islands in the inland waters.

The main watershed is Maan-selkä, which divides the waters flowing into the Baltic Sea from those draining into the Arctic

**Slamom skiing as well as cross country skiing is very popular in Finland.**

**Finland's lakes are an indispensable part of the landscape. In summer, Lake Saimaa, the country's largest waterway (4400 km²), is full of sailing boats and rafts of logs being floated down to the sawmills.**

Ocean and the White Sea. As the snow melts in spring, it flows swiftly down the short river courses and may flood, particularly on the plains along the Gulf of Bothnia coast. The longest river is the Kemijoki (552 km).

**CLIMATE**

The Finnish climate is considerably milder than one might expect from the country's northerly location. The average annual temperature is about 6 degrees Celsius higher than elsewhere in the same latitude. The climate is mitigated by the Baltic Sea, the island waters, but above all by the west winds warmed by the Gulf Stream. In contrast easterly and southerly winds from the Eurasian continent bring cold spells in winter and heat waves in summer: in southern Finland the average temperature in July can be over 20 degrees Celsius and the highest daytime temperature over 30 degrees.

There are major variations in the seasons. Winter is the longest season, and even in the south the day is short, at worst under six hours. In the north the sunless days of *kaamos* time, when even at midday it is dark, last almost six months, but then in summer there can be as many as 70 nightless days. In the south, a midsummer day is only broken as the sun briefly sinks below the horizon and a milky light fills the sky.

Precipitation is even throughout the year, in winter as snow

(some 30–40 % of the total) and in summer as rain. In the south the average annual rainfall is 600 mm/a and in the north 400–500 mm/a. There are about 100 days of rain a year. In midwinter the snow is between 30–40 cm thick in the south and almost 70 cm further north.

**FLORA AND FAUNA**

Most of Finland lies in the northern coniferous forest zone. There are about 1200 species of vascular plants, 800 mosses and over 1000 lichens. Oak grows in the extreme south and southwest of the country, whereas the Lapp fells belong to the Arctic-Alpine zone. Permafrost only occurs in the most northerly swamplands.

The most important natural form of vegetation is the forest, and the most common trees are pine, spruce and birch. There are abundant swamplands, now mostly drained and forested, but considerable areas have been conserved.

The fauna is typical for a northern coniferous zone. Due to strict protective measures the number of major predatory animals has again increased: the bear, wolf, lynx and wolverine live alongside the elk, white-tailed and Finnish deer, and reindeer, the Saimaa seal alongside the beaver. Over 60 spe-cies of mammals have been identified, and the most common in the forests are the squirrel, hare and fox. There are 350 species of birds, most of them migratory, although some like the blackbird

The elk population is considerable, and to keep it in check some 55 000 licenses are issued each year when hunting begins on the 15th October.

The bear, lonely dweller of the wild, north-eastern border areas, wakes in spring from his winter sleep. Bears have increased in numbers and a mature one weighs about 200 kg.

winter in south Finland. The largest birds of prey are the eagle, white-tailed eagle and osprey. There are over 70 species of fish, the most important commercially being the Baltic herring and whitefish. The only poisonous snake in Finland is also the most common;

**The white-tailed eagle was once considered an endangered species, but it is again returning to Finland.**

**Seagulls, once content with the coastal areas, have moved inland and taken over the fields. Another favourite place is Helsinki's market square.**

the now protected viper. There are altogether 11 species of reptiles and frogs.

## CONSERVATION OF NATURE AND THE ENVIRONMENT

The country's most endangered natural resources are its forests and inland waters, both of which are threatened by acid rain which mostly originates from elsewhere. Due to the sharp contrast in seasons, coniferous forests are extremely susceptible. Those in Lapland in particular are now threatened with destruction unless pollution from Russia can be quickly reduced.

The inland waters of south and central Finland are threatened with eutrophication as a result of industrial, urban and agricultural pollution; due to environmental activists this problem is now under control. Conservation of the soil, groundwater, air and the Baltic Sea are other important fields of conservation. Finland has already approved an environment tax in order to incalcate a more environmentally friendly attitude among industrialists and private individuals.

In order to preserve the country's natural environment in its original state, many conservation areas, national parks and wetlands have been established. Some of these have been reserved for research, but most are open to the public and have sign-posted walks.

## ORIGIN OF THE FINNS

Finns in all probability descended from the original settlers that moved into the area after the Ice Age and immigrants from the Baltic region who began arriving about 2000 years ago. Linguistically, Finns, together with the Estonians and Hungarians, belong to the Finno-Ugrian group of languages. Only about 23 million people in the world belong to this group. Finnish differs sharply from European languages. Colonisation from Sweden began in the first millenium AD, first in the Åland Islands, and later along the coastal regions of the Gulf of

11

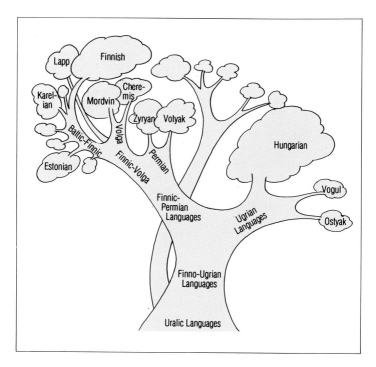

The diagram shows the main Finno-Ugrian languages, spoken by some 23 million people.

Finland and the Gulf of Bothnia.

The official languages of Finland are Finnish and Swedish, the latter nowadays spoken by only 6 % of the population. Other language minorities are the Samis and gipsies. There are about 4400 Lapps, 90 % of whom live in Lapland. The gipsies, numbering about 5500, live mainly in the south.

## POPULATION GROWTH

The first reliable information about the size of the Finnish population dates from the 1750s, when there were slightly less than half a million inhabitants. By 1800 the population was already over 800 000. Population growth in pre-industrial times was very rapid, for by 1870 it had doubled to 1 769 000. Due to improved health conditions and a major decline in the death-rate during the early stages of industrialisation, the population again doubled between 1870 and 1915. After this the birth-rate began to fall slowly, and it was not until after the second world war, at the end of the 1940s, that the population passed the four million mark and finally the 5 million mark in 1992. It has been forecasted, that if the present

**Most Finns have blue or bluish-grey eyes, and fair or brown hair. Z. Topelius, writing in _Suomi 19. vuosisadalla_ (Finland in the 19th century), published in 1898, described the Finns as follows: "The common characteristics are: resilience, inner strength, patience, determination . . . a liking for the old and well-known, and a dislike of the new . . . steadfastness in duty, respect for the law, desire for liberty, honesty . . . a Finn is known for his reserve, for his caution. He needs time to relax and get to know people, but when he does, he is a trustworthy friend . . ."**

birth-rate continues, there will actually be a fall in population. An important influence on population growth has been emigration. Precise figures are not available, but it is estimated that some 250 000 Finns (400 000 including descendents) have permanently emigrated to Sweden, 280 000 to the United States, 20 000 to Canada and 10 000 to Australia.

The average age expectancy for Finnish women is 78 years, for men only 70 years.

## SETTLEMENT

After Iceland and Norway, Finland is the most sparsely inhabited country in Europe. Population density, however, varies considerably. Some 53.5 % of the population lives in the three south-western provinces, occupying only 15 % of the total area of the country. And the population of

13

this area continues to increase rapidly.

This concentration is partly due to the massive process of industrialisation and farm mechanisation that occurred after the second world war. In 1940 some 60 % of the population still derived its livelihood from primary production, yet only 16 % from industry. In the 1950s and 1960s the situation radically changed, and by 1970 the number of those in service trades had risen to almost half, primary production had declined to 20 %, and the share of industry had risen to its present level of about one third. The development of industry and commerce was greatest in the south and southwest, especially in the Greater Helsinki area.

### The ten largest towns in Finland (1.1.1994)

| | |
|---|---|
| Helsinki (Helsingfors) | 501 527 |
| Espoo (Esbo) | 179 067 |
| Tampere (Tammerfors) | 174 861 |
| Turku (Åbo) | 159 916 |
| Vantaa (Vanda) | 159 222 |
| Oulu (Uleåborg) | 103 593 |
| Lahti (Lahtis) | 93 789 |
| Kuopio | 82 341 |
| Pori (Björneborg) | 76 334 |
| Jyväskylä | 71 210 |

(Official Swedish names in brackets)

**The Northern and Southern Esplanades, and the park which lies between them, form one of the most charming areas in Helsinki. The park, one of the oldest in the city, extends from the Market Square to the Swedish Theatre, and has statues to three great poets: J.L. Runeberg, Eino Leino and Zacharias Topelius.**

# A TRAVELLER'S FINLAND

The beauty and pureness of Finland's nature is something remarked on by all visitors to the country. Thousands and thousands of lakes and islands, the archipelago, untouched nature, Lapp fells and rivers, sunlit nightless summers, myriad coloured autumns, "twilight time" in Lapland, snow covered winters, migratory birds returning in spring – all this in a highly industrialised nation whose towns and tourist facilities well equal the standard found elsewhere in Europe. Compared to the countries of Central Europe, Finland remains a clean and peaceful country. The never-ending countryside starts

**A glade of spring wood anemones at Ramsholmen, in the Åland Islands.**

immediately beyond the towns, varying from ancient areas of settlement to untouched wilderness.

If you fly to Finland, the first thing you notice is the extensive archipelago, a jigsaw puzzle of barren skerries and tree-covered islands, then comes the mainland with its mosaic of lakes and islands, fields and forests. Actually, Finland is one of the most forested countries in the world. Apart from the fact that they are an extremely important source of raw material for Finnish industry, forests play an essential part in every Finn's life. The gods of the ancient Finns dwelled in the forest. It provided the raw materials for works of art and handicraft. Whole towns were built from wood and even if many of them have been destroyed by fire, a few idyllic examples remain. Even nowadays wood is one of the most important building materials used in homes and summer cottages, not to mention the hundreds of thousands of saunas. Outside saunas are built wholly from

Huge ships and ferries now ply the ancient Viking route to the east, carrying over 3.5 million passengers a year. Some two million tourists come to Finland every year, over half of them Scandinavians. The picture shows ferries passing each other in the Åland Sea.

Modern legislation allows summer cottages and saunas to be built by the water's edge in certain districts. For many Finns the dream of a cottage by the sea or a lake is already a reality.

timber, those in apartments and houses are at least panelled in wood. Tasty wild berries and mushrooms are picked in large quantities from the forests, providing such culinary delights as lingonberry, cranberry, or rowanberry jelly with game bird or hare, roast venison or elk. Graceful, lichen-patterned silver birches, darkly festive firs, and stately columns of russet-hued pines reflect the different moods of Finland's changing seasons.

If you arrive by ferry or on your own yacht or motorboat, your first acquaintance will be with the countless thousands of islands that constitute the Åland Islands and Saaristomeri, the world of the archipelago. The barren skerries beyond the Åland Islands, Saaristomeri and Helsinki soon give way to pine-covered isles, through which the "floating hotels" ply their way carrying millions of passengers and their cars between Stockholm and Helsinki each year. In summer the journey is an unforgettable experience as the vessel sails the ancient narrow route between the islands in brilliant daylight or summer twilight. And when a Finn returns home in winter on one of these ferries, he normally visits the steaming-hot sauna in the bows below waterlevel, to listen to the crunch of ice against the walls as the ship ploughs its way through the narrow channel kept open in the solid mass of ice.

If you travel by car, train or bus through the lake district, you will discover a unique landscape of thousands of lakes and islands, where the roads are forced to follow the curving shorelines or cut across the narrow straits.

Typical of the inland waterways of Finland is that they form routes that were the most important means of communication before the coming of railways and roads. Even today you can still travel by passenger vessel between the towns of central Finland.

A great number of Finns spend their free time in summer cottages of which there are more than 300 000, usually by a lake, a river or the sea. Others prefer to travel with a caravan, stopping at well-equipped caravan sites and visiting the many attractions of this extensive country. There are also holiday villages nearby many of the most beautiful areas in the country, with well-furnished cottages or cabins for hire. And for those wishing maximum comfort, a high-standard hotel will be found in even the smallest of towns.

Holiday occupations include fishing, rambling, camping in the forests, sailing, gardening, picking berries and mushrooms, and other things that are close to nature. Summer with its "nightless nights" can be quite warm – over 30 degrees Celsius on really hot days – but Finns also enjoy the rich nature of late summer as hundreds of flowers burst into bloom and the air is full of the songs of birds, or the pure, bright colours of early autumn as it changes into the glowing reds and golds of *ruska*. Swimming in the clean rivers, lakes and pools is a natural part of the warmer season, followed naturally by frequent visits to the sauna. But even in winter many Finns take a dip in the ice or roll in the snow after their sauna. A Finnish summer is best enjoyed by a person who both understands and respects nature.

Many consider winter the best season in Finland because it offers a chance to ski. Skiing in the snow-clad forest or in sunlight over an ice-covered lake is a favourite among most Finns. You can cross-country ski almost everywhere and there are slalom slopes even in the most southerly parts of the country. The best time for cross-country skiing in south and central Finland is in March, when the surface of the snow glitters in the rays of the spring sun. The largest ski centres are in Lapland and central Finland. In Lapland the skiing season lasts well into spring, when the sun shines much longer and you can acquire a suntan. In north Lapland, up in Utsjoki, the snow disappears and the nightless summer begins on almost exactly the same day.

In addition to summer, when the sun never goes down and the daytime temperatures are only two-to-three degrees lower than in south Finland, Lapland offers two other quite special seasons, *ruska* and *kaamos*. During *ruska* nature is aflame with quite unbelievable colours. Many return time and time again to admire the colourful symphony of *ruska*, sometimes heightened against the backcloth of the first snows. During *kaamos*, on the other hand, the sun hardly bothers to rise above the horizon. This twilight lasts for only a few hours but, due to the Northern Lights, the bright starlit sky, moonlight and the blanket of pure snow below, a cloudless night offers an exotic and unparalleled experience, enjoyed even by those who have "seen it all". When the heavens retreat behind the clouds and snowflakes begin to fall, it is time to return inside to the warmth of a log fire and listen to Lapp tales.

In addition to the beauty of its nature and countryside, Finland also offers much of historical interest. Hill forts from pagan times, medieval castles from stone and brick, unique folk-built wooden churches and whole wooden towns have been piously preserved. Coastal fishing villages and idyllic inland settlements associated with traditional iron working, wood processing and glass blowing are well worth a visit. New buildings by Finnish architects of international repute also reflect the special characteristics of this northern nation.

**Mid-September is the best time to enjoy the russets of *ruska* at Saariselkä, though both the colours and the time vary from year to year.**

**Utility glassware has been produced in Finland since the end of the 18th century, but the Belgian, French, German and Swedish glassblowers who came here in the following century taught the art of making crystal and decorative glass. Today Finnish design glass has a world reputation.**

Finland is the western gateway to Russia. In addition to flight connections, there are daily trains to St. Petersburg and Moscow, ships sailing to Tallinn, and border crossing points for those travelling by car. There are also trips down the Saimaa Canal to Viipuri. East-West cultural influences, originating from the fact that Finland was first part of Sweden and then of Russia, are particularly apparent in the exciting tensions in Helsinki's townscape.

Political stability and a peaceful way of life, free from the threats of terrorism and violence, have made Finland a popular venue for international conferences, fairs and exhibitions. A flair for organisation and top-level facilities have added to this popularity.

### FINNISH CUISINE

Most Finnish restaurants and cafeterias offer typical international food, and many towns have international fast-food chain outlets. The larger towns also offer a number of national and ethnic restaurants; the Russian ones in Helsinki are really something. Funnily enough, the most difficult thing to find is real Finnish cooking, though local dishes are included in many menus.

Finnish cuisine is based on dairy products, potatoes, meat, fish and bread – dark rye bread, for instance, is for many the ultimate personification of Finnishness. Every county, and many districts even, have their own specialities, which are all worth while trying.

Many of these delights are prepared from such freshwater fish as vendace, whitefish, pike-perch, bream, pike and perch, or sea fish like the Baltic herring, Finland's most important catch. And salmon from Lapland is

A typical smorgasbord groaning with delicacies.

something out of this world. Vendace, whitefish and burbot roe is so exquisite that there is never enough left over for export. It should be mixed with onion and smetana, and washed down with Finlandia or Koskenkorva vodka.

Summer's first delight comes in June; tiny, freshly-dug new potatoes boiled in dill and served with butter and raw herring. In July it's time for wild strawberries and cream, the incomparable blueberry pie, and naturally raspberries. Later come the lingonberries and cranberries, and the rarer cloudberries and arctic brambleberries from which excellent liquers are made. The high point of summer is in August, when one of the world's most succulent freshwater delights is served, the crayfish.

In autumn the forests abound with mushrooms, though the tasty morel is already available in spring. There are literally hundreds of edible mushrooms in Finland, but also a few poisonous ones, so be care- ful and only pick what you recognise. Late autumn restaurants offer such delights as roast elk and occasionally roast bear.

The list of provincial foods and dishes is unending. There are all kinds of pies, including the rice or potato-filled *karjalanpiirakka* and curd-filled cheesecakes from Karelia. Another Karelian dish is *karjalanpaisti*, a casserole of different meats and vegetables. One Savo-Karelian delight is *särä*, lamb slowly roasted on a wooden platter. From Savo, too, comes the famous *kalakukko*, rye bread filled with vendace or perch and pork meat, baked slowly in the oven. Ostrobothnian specialities include *leipäjuusto* cheese made from beestings milk and matured over an open fire, and the unleavened *rieska* bread. To quench one's thirst Häme offers a strong, homemade beer called *sahti*. In Tampere they eat a black *mustamakkara* sausage, in the south-west *rosolli*, a root salad with raw herring, and in Lapland *poronkäristys* from reindeer.

Finnish Christmas starts with cod and continues with roast ham and vegetable casseroles, and Easter with roast lamb followed by *mämmi*, a dessert made from rye and malt. Certain national days have special cakes, such as *runebergintorttu* cake on the national poet Runeberg's day, which should be washed down with a "wee tot", *laskiaispulla* bun on Shrove Tuesday, *tippaleipä* cake with *sima* mead on May Day, and the prune turnover *joulutorttu* at Yuletide.

**Gourmets impatiently await the crayfish season, which starts on 21st July. The crayfish are first boiled in water seasoned with salt and dill, then eaten with traditional ceremony in the company of good friends.**

**Finnish Christmas dinner consists of ham or turkey, vegetable casseroles, herring, salmon and cod.**

## TOURIST AREAS

Finland can be divided into five main tourist areas, each quite different in landscape and culture. They are the south-west, the lake district, Bothnia, east Finland and Lapland.

As Finland's road network and bus system are excellent, all these areas are easily accessible. The rail service extends as far as Rovaniemi in the Arctic Circle and the domestic flight network is very extensive. All transport services offer tourists special season rates, making it possible to travel throughout the country at a reasonable price. The best way to see Finland is by car, and the easiest way to bring it over is by ferry from Sweden, Germany or Poland.

### SOUTH-WEST FINLAND

This is an area of ancient historical settlement and the centre of modern economic life. Industry is concentrated around the new capital Helsinki, and the former capital Turku with its fine historical traditions.

Although history is more strongly evident in the inland rural areas, nature is perhaps at its most beautiful on the coast and archipelago. The Åland Islands and Turku archipelago are a yachtsman's paradise.

**Large crowds line the banks for the annual university rowing race on the Aura at Turku.**

**The idyllic small towns of the southwest are very popular with tourists. The picture shows the well-preserved wooden houses of Old Rauma.**

Between the south-western coast and the Åland Islands lies the Saaristomeri maritime national park.

The largest and most diverse tourist centre is undoubtedly Helsinki, but there are many other interesting and original places in the area that are well worth a visit. Turku with its medieval castle and cathedral, Naantali where a spa has grown up on the site of the monastery of the Order of St. Birgitta, the historic, cathedral town of Porvoo, Hanko for the regatta, Pori for the international jazz festival, Old Rauma with its lovely wooden buildings, and the beautiful port of Mariehamn (Maarianhamina), gateway to the Åland Islands. The coast and the Lohja lake district abound with summer cottages.

The harbour and charming restaurants of Naantali are familiar sights to the thousands of yachtsmen who sail over to visit Finland each year.

## THE LAKE DISTRICT

This is the "Heart of Finland", a land of a thousand lakes flowing down the Kokemäenjoki, Kymijoki and Vuoksi rivers to the Baltic Sea. The main lakes are Saimaa, Päijänne, Vanajavesi and Näsijärvi, and the best way to see them is from one of the ships plying between the towns. The main tourist centre is Tampere, closely followed by Savonlinna, Mikkeli, Lappeenranta, Imatra and the winter sports citadel of Lahti. The most famous natural attraction is the Punkaharju ridge formed during the Ice Age. Another place of interest to visitors is the Orthodox monastery and convent at Heinävesi.

## BOTHNIA

The main tourist centres along the Bothnian coast and the low-

For more than a century the landscape around Koli has been the most important tourist attraction of North Karelia. It inspired this painting by Pekka Halonen.

lying farmlands of west Finland are Vaasa, Kalajoki and Oulu. Vaasa and Tornio are important crossing points to Sweden. The Kaustinen Folk Music Festival is the cultural event that most interests travellers in the area.

## EAST FINLAND

This sparsely-inhabited area bordering on Russia is a kind of in-between zone between the lake district and Lapland. Its largely untouched nature is studded with clear lakes, streams and forested fells. Karelian and

Imatrankoski rapids are not only a fantastic sight, but a major producer of hydro-electricity. During the summer the rapids roar for about 20 minutes a day.

Orthodox cultural traditions are strongest in the southern part, around Joensuu and Ilomantsi, nearby Finland's most famous and pictureseque sight, the Koli Heights above Lake Pielisjärvi. Along the Bard and Border Way the traveller passes through areas associated with the national epic poem *Kalevala* and the battlegrounds of the last war. To the north, in Kainuu and Kuusamo, the landscape begins to look like Lapland, and offers the opportunity for hiking in the wilderness or shooting the rapids. This is an ideal place in winter for skiing and slaloming.

## LAPLAND

The very location of Lapland in and north of the Arctic Circle is exotic. Many come here to see the midnight sun or experience *kaamos* in wintertime. Others are attracted by the open fells, autumnal *ruska*, the lure of gold-panning, angling the ice-cold streams, hiking in the wilderness, cross-country skiing in late winter and early spring, and naturally everything associated with the Lapp way of life and reindeers.

Most travellers pass through Rovaniemi, the gateway to Lapland, as they make their way along the few but highly scenic roads in this region. The largest tourist centre, Saariselkä, is in the Urho Kekkonen National Park. There are several other national parks in Lapland, the most important for visitors are those at Pallas-Ounastunturi and Lemmenjoki.

### THE RIGHTS AND DUTIES OF TOURISTS

Camping and caravaning should normally be in the numerous and well-equipped camping sites. Camping out is permitted in certain areas, provided campers observe strict rules of cleanliness and in no way spoil surrounding nature. Hikers should note that nature is untamed, so they should be properly equipped and carry map and compass.

As nature is highly vulnerable, tourists should follow all rules and regulations, and be especially careful not to disturb reindeer. Felling trees, even dead ones, is a punishable offence. Detailed instructions
for hikers are available from all tourist centres.

Information concerning passports and visas, work and residence permits, is available from all tourist organisations and authorities. Most foreign visitors do not require a visa.

### IMPORTANCE OF THE TOURIST INDUSTRY

The majority of visitors to Finland come from Scandinavia, Germany, the United States, the United Kingdom and Russia. Tourism accounts for about 3 % of total Finnish exports of goods and services, slightly more than in other highly industrialised countries, but considerably less than in the major tourist nations of southern Europe. The share of tourism in the gnp is about

1 %. The tourist industry gives full-time employment to some 69 000~70 000 people as well as to a large number of seasonal workers.

### TOURIST AUTHORITIES AND ORGANISATIONS
There are innumerable offices and organisations throughout Finland catering for tourists. Nationally, the most important is the Ministry of Trade and Industry's Finnish Tourist Board (MEK), which has offices abroad, and the Finnish Tourist Association, which is responsible for publishing tourist guides.

**It is easy to become bewitched by Lapland as one skiis over the sparkling snow under a brilliant spring sun.**

In the larger centres there are tourist offices, and many districts have their own tourist manager or officer responsible for developing and co-ordinating local tourism.

## CONSTITUTION AND FORM OF GOVERNMENT

On the 6.12.1917 Finland declared its independence from Russia, which had become a Soviet Republic on 7.11.1917. For over a century before, Finland had been a Grand Duchy within the Russian Empire, an autonomous state with its own constitution and form of government.

In autumn 1917 the Senate presented Parliament with the proposal that Finland become a sovereign republican state. This was approved on 6.12.1917 and recognised by the Soviet government under V.I. Lenin on 4.1.1918. The constitution of the republic came into force in July 1919 after the form of state had been decided upon. The other important constitutional law is the Parliament Act, enacted in its present form in 1928. Since this time there have been no essential changes to the country's constitution.

The constitution lays down the rules concerning the form and powers of the highest organs of the state, as well as the constitutional rights of its citizens, who are equal before the law. Ultimate power is vested in the people as represented by Parliament. Parliament Act specifies in detail the structure and duties of Parliament and the electoral system. The 200 members of Parliament are elected by direct vote for a period of four years, but the president of the republic has the right to dissolve Parliament before the end of this period and order new elections. The country is divided into 14 electoral districts, from which members are elected to Parliament by the d'Hondt system of proportional representation. The self-governing province of the Åland Islands elects one member. Parliament exercises its legislative authority in conjunction with the president, who has the power to initiate legislation and give his consent to laws. Parliament gives its approval to the government's budget proposal and supervises the work of the government.

## THE PRESIDENT OF THE REPUBLIC

According to the constitution, the highest executive power in the country is vested in the president, who is elected for a period of six years at a time. The president is chosen by direct election, with a run-off in case no candidate gets an absolute majority on the first ballot.

The formal powers vested in

**The picture shows the colourful garden of Kultaranta, the president's summer residence in Naantali.**

the president are very extensive. He decides on the presentation of government legislative proposals to Parliament, he gives his consent to laws or exercises his temporary right of veto, issues statutes, calls emergency sittings of Parliament, declares elections, presides over the opening and closing of Parlia- ment, appoints senior civil servants and judges, determines foreign policy and is commander-in-chief of the armed forces. With rare exceptions, the president only exercises his power through the Council of State, over which he presides. The chancellor of justice, who is present at meetings of the Council of State, is responsible for the legality of its decisions. The Council of State is responsible for the decisions of the president.

## THE COUNCIL OF STATE AND THE ADMINISTRATION

The president of the republic appoints the prime minister and his ministers, who must be native-born Finns. Ministers and the Council of State must enjoy the confidence of Parliament. Thus although the Council of State is politically responsible to Parliament, the president is not. The president resides over those

**Party election posters, with Helsinki Cathedral in the background.**

meetings of the Council of State in which the matters dealt with come within his powers – at which time one talks of government – otherwise the council meets under the leadership of the prime minister. The president is not bound to consider the opinions of the prime minister or even the majority of the Council of State, although in practice he almost invariably does so. Although over the decades the exercise of presidential power has varied in accordance with the character of the incumbent, the Finnish political system has remained parliamentary.

There are 12 ministries under the Council of State, each with its own field of responsibility. Due to the division of the tasks of certain ministries between two ministers,

the Council of State at present consists of the prime minister and 17 ministers. Matters of major importance are decided at council meetings, minor issues are left to the ministers.

The Council of State and the ministries are responsible only for the major affairs of state. Several ministries have boards under them in which authority is wielded by a collegiate of senior civil servants.

The country is divided into 12 provinces, each with its own government led by a governor appointed by the president. The provincial government is responsible for local adminis-tration and other regional tasks. It is, for example, the highest police authority in the area. Provincial governments are responsible for the local government authorities, the 224 districts under their sheriffs, and the magistrates in the so-called "ancient cities".

Historically, the Åland Islands occupy a special position because, since the Crimean War of 1856, they have been declared an unfortified area in international law. Moreover, they are almost totally Swedish-speaking. Since 1920 they have possessed a large measure of self-government, most recently reaffirmed in 1951. Laws of a constitutional nature may not be changed or repealed without the approval of the 30-member Provincial Parliament chosen at a general election. The islands are administered by a govern-ment of seven under the chair-manship of the provincial president, the highest official being the governor.

Central and local government are separated, and the country is divided into 460 municipalities, of which 97 are towns.

### POLITICAL PARTIES

Parties are the very foundation of Finnish political life. At the last general election, members of Parliament were elected from nine different party lists. The parties represent different sections of society and opinions, campaign fiercely in local, general and presidential elections, and fill administrative positions from which their representatives exert political power.

Although political life since the end of the war has been characterised by a prolonged struggle between the country-side and the towns, this never prevented the Agrarian Party (nowadays the Centre Party KESK) and the urban-based Social Democratic Party (SDP) from forming coalition govern-ments with the support of other smaller parties. In 1987, however, after decades in opposition, the conservative National Coalition Party (KOK) replaced the Centre Party and formed a government with the SDP. After the 1991 elections the Centre Party formed

**Party support in the 1991 parliamentary elections**

|  | % of votes | Seats |
|---|---|---|
| Centre Party (KESK) | 24.8 | 55 |
| Finnish Social Democratic Party (SDP) | 22.1 | 48 |
| National Coalition Party (KOK) | 19.3 | 40 |
| League of the Left (Vas.) | 10.1 | 19 |
| Swedish People's Party (SFP/RKP) | 5.5 | 12 |
| Greens (Vihreät) | 6.8 | 10 |
| Finnish Rural Party (SMP) | 4.8 | 7 |
| Finnish Christian League (SKL) | 3.1 | 8 |
| Liberal People's Party (LKP) | 0.8 | 1 |

Åland Coalition (Åländsk Samling):
1 seat included in the National Coalition Party list

a goverment with the National Coalition Party as its main partner.

Ever since independence, Parliament has almost always had a non-socialist majority. As the number of white-collar workers has increased, so has support for the traditional conservative KOK. Support for KESK came mainly from the farmers, but with urban migration the party has now gained a foothold in the towns. Their strongholds, however, are still in north and east. The liberal Swedish People's Party (RKP) mainly draws its voters from the Swedish-speaking minority. The popularist Finnish Rural Party (SMP), which split off from the Agrarian Party in 1959, has based itself around the issue of the "forgotten" rural poor. The Finnish Christian League (SKL), which like its fellow parties in the rest of Scandinavia draws support from the free church, gained its first seat in 1970.

The Greens entered Parliament in 1983, but the group has now split into two wings. The left is represented by the SDP and the League of the Left.

In 1990, the long-divided Finnish Communist Party (SKP) decided to disband itself and reform as the League of the Left, a forum for all dissenting groups of the far left.

**LOCAL GOVERNMENT**

The constitution grants local government extensive powers. Municipalities are responsible for the administration of their localities independently of the state and for carrying out such duties otherwise prescribed for by law. They are thus responsible for schools, hospitals and health centres, town planning and social welfare. Although they have the right to levy taxes on

**Helsinki City Hall houses the offices and chambers of the city board. In front soldiers on their way to the changing of the guard.**

those living within the area, they also receive assistance from the central government in proportion to their means. In return the state possesses considerable powers of control over the activities of local authorities, which naturally diminishes their autonomy. Every effort is being made to increase self-government, and a "free-municipality" experiment has been introduced which gives the relevant localities a broad measure of economic independence.

The highest decision-making body in local government is the municipal council, elected by direct, proportional representation, with 17 to 85 members depending on the population of the municipality. This allows quite small groups to be represented. Councils elect their own chairman, and appoint an executive body, the municipal board, for a period of two years at a time. Councils also appoint a number of statutory and voluntary committees to carry out administrative tasks. Because of the proportional system of election, party strengths in councils are also reflected in the committees. The representation of women in these organs is guaranteed by law. Tens of thousands of citizens throughout the country are involved in the work of local government.

The highest local government officer is the municipal or town manager, who is appointed by the council and is directly responsible to the board.

There are about 400 inter-municipal unions in the country for co-operation and coordination in such fields as hospitals, trade schools or regional planning.

## THE JUDICIARY

The independence of the courts in Finland is guaranteed by the constitution, for it is virtually impossible to remove judges and the judiciary plays a paramount role in their appointment.

There are three levels of courts in civil and criminal cases: those of first instance are the circuit courts and in the "old cities" the city courts, the next instance is the Court of Appeal, and the highest instance is the Supreme Court. Within the provinces, administrative cases are tried by county administrative courts from which appeal is to the Supreme Administrative Court. Other special courts include the housing, insurance, land rights, water rights and appeals, and market courts and the High Court of Impeachment.

The only link between the judiciary and the political system is that the president appoints the presidents and members of the Supreme Court and Supreme Administrative Court on the basis of the recommendations of the courts. The Supreme Court appoints the judges to the circuit courts, as well as the chairmen of the city courts, the other members being appointed by ancient right by the municipal councils. The highest public prosecutor is the Chancellor of Justice, under whom are the provincial police superinten-dents, sheriffs and municipal public prosecutors. The prison department of the Ministry of Justice is responsible for carrying out prison sentences, its bailiffs enforce judgements in lawsuits and collect fines, tax arrears and debts.

The highest law officer in the state is the chancellor of justice, who is appointed by the presi-dent. He participates at meetings of the government and ensures that the authorities observe the laws and fulfil their duties. Parliament chooses an ombuds-man, who ensures that courts and civil servants observe the law. Citizens have the right to appeal to either of them if they feel they have suffered injustice at the hands of the authorities.

A new practice has been introduced in several districts whereby a conciliation office endeavours to bring about an agreement out of court between young offenders and their victims, thus preventing the former commencing on a career of recidivism. Community work for offenders is also being introduced.

# HISTORY

### PREHISTORY

The first people reached Finland shortly after the end of the last Ice Age, when the glaciers had retreated and the land risen above the sea. On the basis of their race and language, they are assumed to have belonged to the Fenno-Ugrian family. They mainly hunted and fished the coastal areas, and it was not until the beginning of the present era that these people from south of the Gulf of Finland gave this land and nation its name. There is evidence of Stone Age (c. 7500–1500 BC) occupation as far north as the Arctic Circle, though it was mainly concentrated along the coast. During the Bronze Age (c. 1500–500 BC) and Iron Age (c. 500 BC–1150/1300 AD) settlers moved inland, trading and establishing cultural links with both West and East. During the Viking period, there were close contacts with Scandinavia and Russia. When, after their conversion to Christianity, Scandinavians ceased their long-distance raiding, the Finnish and Baltic pagans carried on plundering.

It is believed that the Sampo story in the *Kalevala* is based on the tales handed down by these pagan plunderers.

### THE SWEDISH PERIOD
### (c. 1200–1809)

At the beginning of historical time, Finland was still divided

**This 5000-year-old elk head weapon was found in southwest Finland, and many similar ones have been found elsewhere.**

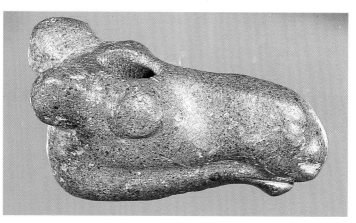

The ironmaster's manor of Fagervik (the main building dates from 1773), in the western part of Uusimaa, was one of the early centres of metalworking and market gardening in Finland.

into different and often hostile tribal areas. During the 12th century voyages were even made to Finland from Denmark and Sweden as part of the traditional Road to the East. Up to this time Finland was a political vacuum of interest both to its western neighbour Sweden and the Roman Catholic Church and its eastern neighbour Novgorod (Russia) and the Greek Orthodox Church. The emerging Swedish state tried to establish its old relationship with Finland. The Finns in the southwest and Häme oriented themselves to the West, those in Karelia to the East. Christianity reached western Finland in the middle of the 12th century, that is, before the first crusade there. Some kind of union was thought to exist between Sweden and Finland. Not until 1216 did the Pope confirm the right of the Swedish king to this area, after which the process of conquest and conversion continued into Häme, Uusimaa and Karelia, where a castle was built at Viipuri. Under the Treaty of Pähkinäsaari, signed between Sweden and Novgorod in 1323, the most eastern part of Karelia was ceded to Novgorod, so dividing the Karelian tribe between two kingdoms. West and south Finland remained within the western cultural sphere, and part of Karelia came under the influence of Russia and Byzantine. Thus Finland became an integral part of the Swedish state.

**Albert Edelfelt's painting The Inauguration of the Royal Academy of Turku in 1640.**

Under the influence of Sweden, the Scandinavian legal and social systems took root in Finland. Power was centred in the 13th-century town of Turku, which in time came to be protected by a magnificent castle. Turku was also the episcopal see, and the first Finnish bishop, Maunu I, was appointed in 1291. It was the church that tied Finland to the mainstream of European culture. In 1362 it was noted that Finland had the right to send representatives to the royal elections, and this it did following the establishment of a Diet of the Four Estates in Sweden in the 16th century. The Reformation reached Finland at the same time as elsewhere in Scandinavia, in the first half of the 16th century.

During Sweden's great power period (1617–1721), it controlled the whole of the Baltic region and steadily pushed the eastern border of Finland further and further east. It was Finland, that suffered most from military action in this era, a plight worsened by severe famine in 1696–1697 when almost a third of the population perished from hunger or disease. Sweden also tightened her control over the province during this era, bringing Finnish administration and conditions into conformity with the mother country. Swedes were appointed to the highest offices, the importance of Swedish increased and a process of "Swedification" was carried out to the severe impediment of the fledgling Fennophile movement.

The foundation of Finland's first university, Åbo Academy (nowadays the University of Helsinki), in 1640 did much to advance the academic life of the country, despite the dominance of Swedish.

The end of Sweden as a great power came in the Great Northern War of 1700–1721 with the Russian occupation of Finland in 1714, when the Swedish army was preoccupied on the Continent. This was followed by the period of the Great Wrath, which finished with the Peace of Uusikaupunki in 1721 under which southeast Finland was ceded to Russia. During the Russian War of 1741–1743 the Swedish-Finnish army was defeated and surrendered, and Russia again occupied Finland (the Lesser Wrath). Although Russia agreed to withdraw its troops at the Peace of Turku in 1743, the price was further territorial concessions; the eastern border was pushed even further west. Even at this time it was suggested in Finland that the country should separate from Sweden.

Over the following decades the government paid special attention to improving the country's economy and defences. In 1747 work began on Viapori (Sveaborg), an island fortress just off Helsinki. This, the strongest of its kind in the region, a "Gibraltar of the North", was soon followed by a powerful coastal navy. The reign of Gustavus III (1771–1792) saw great improvements in the government and economy of Finland, and many new towns were established. During the 1788–1790 war against Russia, a separist movement began among army officers, which did not, however, receive much support among the populace. Separatism had, however, some effect on Russian behaviour at the end of the next war.

### THE AUTONOMOUS GRAND DUCHY OF FINLAND (1809–1917)

In 1807 Napoleon and Alexander I agreed at Tilsit, that Russia would force Sweden to join the continental blockade against Great Britain. When diplomatic pressure failed, Russia attacked Finland, and in the 1808–1809 war defeated its army and

Emanuel Thelning's painting of Alexander I opening the first Finnish Diet in 1809.

occupied the country. Unlike the two previous wars in 1721 and 1743, this time Russia did not withdraw. A peace was signed in 1809 under which Finland was ceded by Sweden to Russia. The importance of Finland to Russia can be understood when considering the defence of St. Petersburg.

The tsar had already decreed that the affairs of Finland were to come under his direct jurisdiction. At the session of the Finnish Diet in Porvoo in 1809, Finns swore their allegiance to the tsar, who in return promised to respect their Evangelical-Lutheran faith, constitutional laws and rights, stating that Finland now belonged to the family of nations.

In being joined to Russia, Finland became an autonomous Grand Duchy, with the tsar its constitutional monarch as represented by a governor-general. The highest organ of government was the Senate, whose members were Finns, and in theory the country had its own Diet of the Four Estates. Thus a separate Finnish state came into being complete with its own institutions.

All major decisions concerning Finland had to be subjected to the tsar, and were presented to him by the Finnish representative at the court of St. Petersburg. A direct contact with the tsar was thus established, so the affairs of the Grand Duchy were not managed via the Russian authorities. The tsar gave every encouragement to the country in order to weaken Swedish influence. The network of canals and roads was improved, Helsinki became the new capital, and work began on providing it with buildings of unprecedented beauty. Most of these still exist, often housing the same state organs.

Finnish national consciousness was strengthened during the period of autonomy: Lönnrot compiled the epic saga *Kalevala*, and the patriotic poetry of Runeberg was hailed with enthusiasm. Snellman, the great statesman and thinker of the period, fought for equality between Finnish and Swedish as the official languages of the nation. Finnish-speaking grammar schools were established. Snellman was most active during the time of Alexander II (1855–1881), when he was a senator and professor at the University of Helsinki.

The national movement gave rise to parties based on language, first the Fennomans in the 1860s and in the following decade the Svecomans. By the end of the century the Finnish side had emerged victorious, helped considerably by the fact that only one in seven of the population spoke Swedish as their mother tongue.

Finland's special status was first questioned by the extremist

**The Great Strike in autumn 1905 was Finland's protest against tsarist oppression, and resulted in a new, unicameral parliament elected by proportional representation. Soon after relations between the right and the left so deteriorated that an armed conflict between the Whites and the Reds broke out.**

Pan-Slavists during the reign of Alexander III (1881–1894), and later, under the weak rule of Nicholas II (1894–1917), the Russians began to systematically undermine the country's autonomy. The February Manifesto of 1899 so limited the authority of the Finnish Diet that one could talk about a usurpation of power. This led to an unprecedented protest movement,

or merely defend the position of Finnish. The Finnish Party, particularly the reactionary Old Finns, chose the latter conciliatory path, whereas the Young Finns and the greater part of the organised labour movement opted for opposing all illegal measures on constitutional grounds.

Russia's defeat in the war against Japan in 1905 resulted in a general strike which soon spread to Finland and forced the tsar to liberalise his regime. A radical parliamentary reform was carried out in Finland in 1906, with the introduction of a unicameral parliament, and universal and equal suffrage. The most progressive act was the extension of the franchise to women, the first in Europe to gain full political rights. A new wave of oppression soon began (1908–1914) that went as far as russifying the Senate. Finland's position was reinstated after the February Revolution in Russia in 1917.

culminating in the collection within ten days of over half a million signatures on a petition to the tsar. This, like another from over a thousand Europeans prominent in cultural life, failed to have any effect. The first period of oppression began. No longer was language the great divider, but the attitude to Russia. The main question was whether to resist all forms of russification

### INDEPENDENT FINLAND
### (1917 onwards)

With the outbreak of the First world war, the separatist movement strengthened in Finland, underground activities flourished, and young men left in secret to acquire military training abroad in preparation for an armed struggle.

Following the October Revolution the Senate under

Marshal Carl Gustaf Emil Mannerheim (1867–51) is one of the most important figures in Finnish history. During the Civil War he was commander of the White forces and in 1918 was appointed head of state. During the Winter and Continuation wars he was again commander-in-chief of the armed forces. It was due to him that Finland stood her ground and peace was achieved, albeit on harsh terms. He was also president for a brief period in 1944. The portrait is by Akseli Gallen-Kallela.

P.E. Svinhufvud declared Finland independent on 6 December 1917 and this was recognised by Soviet Russia on 4 January 1918. However, the radical wing of the Social Democratic Party, the Reds, wished to carry out a Russian-style revolution in Finland. The revolution began in January 1918, with the Reds taking over the whole of south Finland and forcing the Senate to flee to Vaasa. The Civil War, in which the government, the Whites, received help from the Kaiser's Germany and the Reds from Bolshevik Russia, ended in May 1918 with the victory of the White forces under Lt. General Gustaf Mannerheim. This was similarly a war of independence because the Russian troops stationed in Finland were expelled from the country. With the collapse of Germany in November 1918, Finland switched over from an active pro-German policy and turned towards the Allies. The parliamentary system approved of in 1919, a compromise between republican and monarchist interests, gave the President of the Republic a dominant position. He was responsible for foreign policy, was commander-in-chief of the armed forces, and had the right to dismiss parliament.

In spring 1919, largely due to the personal influence of Mannerheim who was at that time head of state, Finnish independence was recognised by Great Britain and the United States. The same year K.J. Stålberg was elected the first president of the Finnish republic.

In 1920 relations with Soviet Russia were normalised when the two nations signed the Peace of Tartu.

In the early 1920s Parliament busied itself legislating for the new republic. Laws were passed concerning freedom of religion, compulsory elementary education, military service, freedom of speech and association, land reform, and prohibition (repealed in 1932). The participation of the Social Democrats in government between 1926–1927 did much to heal the wounds of the Civil War. However, in 1929 the Lapua Movement, modelled on the Italian Fascists, demanded the suppression of Communist activities and forced Parliament to pass the so-called Communist Law in 1930. The Lapua Movement was outlawed in 1932 following an unsuccessful armed putsch. The language question reared its head again during the 1920s, this time the struggle centred around the University of Helsinki where not all subjects were yet taught in Finnish. It was not until the end of the following decade that a final compromise was reached.

Foreign policy was based on collaboration with Poland and the Baltic countries, the fringe

**Changes in Finland's eastern frontiers:**
1. 1323–1617
2. 1809–1920
3. since 1944

nations who had separated from Russia. From the outset, the cornerstone of its security policy was the League of Nations. When, by 1935, this body had proved itself unable to maintain world peace, Finland issued a declaration that from now on its security would be based on an orientation towards Scandinavia.

The Soviet Union did not accept this and its suspicions of Finnish intentions grew as the European situation worsened. It demanded that Finland cede certain areas in order to strengthen the strategic defence of Leningrad. This the Finnish government did not agree to. In August 1939 the Soviet Union had signed a Non-Aggression Pact with Germany, the secret protocols of which proved incidental to the outbreak of the second world war. At the end of November 1939 the Soviet Union renounced its 1932 Non-Aggression Pact with Finland and commenced hostilities. The Winter War ended with the Peace of Moscow signed the following

**In the Winter War Finland fought the Soviet Union alone for three and a half months under exacting conditions, yet survived as an independent nation.**

**In 1975, the heads of 35 nations signed the final document of the CSCE conference in Helsinki. The same spirit of Helsinki symbolised the gulf crisis summit meeting in autumn 1990. The photo, taken in the yellow room at the President's Palace, shows Mrs Raisa Gorbachev, President Mikhail Gorbachev, Mrs Tellervo Koivisto, President Mauno Koivisto, Mrs Barbara Bush and President George Bush.**

March. Though fighting alone Finland had managed to preserve her independence, but at the cost of surrendering the Karelian Isthmus and the outer islands of the Gulf of Finland to the Soviet Union.

Despite the peace treaty, the Soviet Union continued to exert pressure on Finland, whose fears grew when the Baltic states were forcibly incorporated into the USSR in August 1940. Isolated from the West and with Sweden staunchly neutral, Finland turned towards Germany. When the Nazis invaded the Soviet Union in June 1941, Finland followed suit. To have remained outside would probably have led to the occupation of the country by one or other of the belligerents. Thus began the Continuation War, and by autumn 1941 Finnish troops had penetrated deep into east Karelia beyond the old border. Thereafter the front line stabilised until the Russians began their massive counter-offensive in summer 1944, forcing the Finns to sue for peace. Under the terms of the armistice dictated by the Soviets in Moscow in September 1944, Finland's eastern border reverted to that of 1940, Petsamo was ceded, and heavy war reparations imposed. As the German forces in Lapland refused to leave voluntarily, Finland was ordered to drive them out in a bitter war that terminated in spring 1945. The Paris Peace Treaty of 1947 confirmed the terms of the Moscow armistice, which included the leasing of Porkkala, a coastal area near Helsinki, to the Soviet Union, and the heavy burden of war reparations which Finland alone among all nations paid on time.

J.K. Paasikivi succeeded Marshal Mannerheim as president in 1946. His goal was to create a new relationship with the Soviet Union based on peace and trust. In 1947 the Allied Control Commission left Finland, and the following year a Treaty of Friendship, Co-operation and Mutual Assistance was concluded with the USSR. (It was in force until the disintegration of the Soviet Union in 1991.)

Over the following years, Finnish foreign policy stabilised and the opportunities for consolidating the Paasikivi Line improved. Largely due to the effect of reparations, the structure of the economy underwent a radical change. Payment was completed in 1952, the same year as the Olympic Games were held in Helsinki. In 1955 the Soviet Union terminated its 50-year lease on Porkkala, returning the area to Finland. The same year Finland became a member of the United Nations and the Nordic Council.

The election of Urho Kekkonen as president in 1956 further strengthened Finland's policy of active neutrality. In 1962 Finland became an associate member of EFTA and in 1973 signed a free-trade agreement with the EEC. Finland joined the European Economic Area (EEA) in 1993. The European Union and Finland signed a treaty of accession in Corfu in June 1994 and in October 1994 the "yeses" carried the day in a consultative referendum. Finland will thus become a full member in the beginning of 1995 after the parliaments have ratifier the treaty of accession.

Urho Kekkonen resigned in 1981 and the following year Mauno Koivisto was elected president. Finland also hosted the CSCE follow-up summit in 1992 in a totally changed world as the Soviet Union had disintegrated the year before.

In 1994 Martti Ahtisaari was elected president.

### The presidents of Finland

| | |
|---|---|
| K.J. Stålberg | 1919–1925 |
| Lauri Kr. Relander | 1925–1931 |
| P.E. Svinhufvud | 1931–1937 |
| Kyösti Kallio | 1937–1940 |
| Risto Ryti | 1940–1944 |
| Carl Gustaf Mannerheim | 1944–1946 |
| J.K. Paasikivi | 1946–1956 |
| Urho Kekkonen | 1956–1981 |
| Mauno Koivisto | 1982–1994 |
| Martti Ahtisaari | 1994– |

# FOREIGN POLICY

Sweden's and Finland's common history, and the fact that Swedish is Finland's second official language, have helped forge strong ties with the other Nordic nations. The heads of state frequently visit their neighbouring countries. In the picture, their royal highnesses Carl Gustaf and Silvia of Sweden are with President Martti Ahtisaari and Mrs Eeva Ahtisaari in Stockholm in 1994.

Finland's foreign policy rapidly consolidated after the war and won the unanimous support of all sections of the population. According to the constitution, foreign policy is initiated by the president. Political parties participate in the making of foreign policy when their representatives

are in office and sit in the Council of State over which the president presides. The main goal of Finland's foreign policy, like that of any other country, is to ensure the security and independence of the nation and the wellbeing of its citizens. Its content and methods are based on Finland's own experience and needs.

## FINLAND AND THE OTHER NORDIC NATIONS

As one of the five Nordic countries, Finland naturally identifies herself with them. They are all small nations, with similar social systems and exercising a high degree of collaboration. Denmark has long been member of the European Union. The other four have been members of EFTA and the European Economic Area (EEA). EU and Finland signed a treaty of accession in 1994 and the Finnish people voted in favour of membership in October 1994. After the ratification of the treaty of accession by the parliament Finland will become a member of EU in 1995. A refe-rendum on membership will be carried out before the end of the year in Sweden and Norway.

Many joint organs, such as the consultative Nordic Council and Nordic Council of Ministers, are responsible for the continuous development of inter-Nordic co-operation and integration. Nordic citizens may travel and work freely throughout the area without need of passports or labour permits. They enjoy almost the same social benefits as the citizens of the country in which they are residing. Nordic co-operation contains no supra-national intentions, as each state retains its own sovereignty.

The Nordic countries have much in common in the sphere of foreign policy. This can be seen in their behaviour in the United Nations and other international bodies, as well as their stand on disarmament, aiding the developing countries and other forms of international co-operation, where they often act in consort. The groundwork for international collaboration is prepared at twice-annual meetings of the Nordic foreign ministers.

### FINLAND AND RUSSIA

In 1809 the Russian tsar Alexander I seized Finland from the Swedes and converted the coun-try into an autonomous grand duchy under his direct jurisdiction. During almost a century of imperial rule, Finland's national development was marked by increasing prosperity. However, as Russia's internal difficulties multiplied towards the end of the 19th century, so Finland's position also worsened. When in 1917 the Bolsheviks ceased power in Russia, Finland declared itself independent. During the 1920s and 1930s relations between the young

According to the Finnish constitution, the president occupies a central position with wide powers in foreign policy. State visits have become increasingly important. The picture is from the visit by President Ahtisaari and Mrs Eeva Ahtisaari to Russia. Their hosts were President Boris Yeltsin and Mrs Yeltsin.

republic and the bolshevik Soviet Union were hostile. Following the signing of the Non-Aggression Pact between Russia and Germany in 1939, the secret protocol which placed Finland within Stalin's sphere of influence, the country was attacked by the Soviet Union. From 1939 to 1945 the country was embroiled in the maelstrom of the second world war, fighting the Winter and Continuation wars against the Russians and then against the Ger-mans in Lapland. Although the great power won, Finland was never conquered or occupied.

The Paris Peace Treaty that terminated the second world war created the basis for the development of relations between Finland and the Soviet Union. Another major landmark was the Treaty of Friendship, Co-operation and Mutual Assistance signed in 1948. This marked the beginning of improved and friendly relations between the two countries, as it guaranteed the security of the northwestern border of the otherwise suspicious Soviet Union. This treaty was in force until the disintegration of the Soviet Union in 1991.

Relations between Finland and the successor of the USSR, CIS, have continued to be good. Trade has begun to grow again after the downturn at the beginning of the 1990s and Finland is doing its best to collaborate with Russia in such projects as the moderni-sation of its mining and metal industries. Numerous joint venture companies have been set up in different branches of the economy. The number of Russian tourists visiting Finland has also greatly increased.

## RELATIONS WITH OTHER COUNTRIES

A centuries old tradition links Finland via the Baltic to the rest of what is, geographically, overseas western Europe. The Baltic Sea has offered a channel for the development of cultural relations, trade and tourism, a function by no means diminished by the growth of air traffic and information communications. The Conference on Security and Co-operation in Europe, the final document which was signed in Helsinki in 1975, was of major importance, as was the follow-up conference in 1992.

In its foreign trade policy Finland has aimed at protecting its own interests whilst working for the all-round elimination of trade barriers. A member of EFTA, GATT/WTO and EEA, Finland will become a full member of the European Union in 1995. Through its membership of the Council of Europe Finland participates in the EUREKA Project and is a member of the European Space Agency.

Finland has traditionally enjoyed close and amicable relations with the USA and Canada, the two non-European participants in the CSCE process. In recent years the country has extended its commercial and diplomatic representation throughout Asia, Africa and Latin America.

In recent decades Finland has been active in development co-operation, allocating generous sums from its budget to pro-grammes initiated by inter-national bodies, as well as joint Nordic projects in Africa. With the recession of the early 1990s, however, the sums have not been quite so lavish as before. The main recipients of its own development programmes are Tanzania, Zambia, Vietnam, Kenya, Egypt and Sri Lanka. And like other nations it also has its own individual development projects. Finland has been one of the most active contributors to the UN peace keeping forces, and its latest effort is to help in the peace keeping mission in the former Yugoslavia.

For a long time now one of the main objectives of Finnish foreign policy has been disarmament. Since the end of the second world war, she has been a party to all the relevant disarmament agreements. Finland has been particularly active in promoting the limitation and control of nuclear and other weapons of

Finnish peacekeeping troops in
Namibia before she became
independent.

mass destruction. She has also strongly supported the international control system created by the 1968 Non-Proliferation of Nuclear Weapons Treaty, worked to extend the Nuclear Test Ban Treaty of 1963 to cover underground tests, and participated in international seismological monitoring. A further contribution in this field was by offering Helsinki as the venure for the preliminary negotiations between the great powers that resulted in the START 1 agreement of 1972. In world efforts to restrict chemical weapons, Finland has taken part in an international project to develop methods of control.

### FINLAND AND THE UNITED NATIONS

Ever since Finland became a member of the UNO in 1955, she has actively participated in the work of that organisation, its commissions, bodies and agencies, and the conferences it has arranged. Though supporting UN aims, principles and efforts to promote international security, Finland has understood the limitations and difficulties the organisation faces. In its efforts to promote peaceful settlements, human rights, economic and social progress, self-determination and international law, the United Nations furthers international security and protects the interests of small countries such as Finland. For this reason Finland has made every effort to strengthen the organisation. Conscious of her duty as a developed and affluent industrial nation, Finland has continuously increased her contribution to UN development co-operation, refugee and relief programmes. Unfortunately, due to the world – wide economic recession, Finland was forced to decrease its contribution.

The UN has generally turned to the smaller, neutral nations to

**Finland has widely participated in international development projects. These textbooks for Namibian schools, written and illustrated by Namibian scholarship holders, were produced and printed in Finland.**

supply the soldiers for its peace-keeping forces, and Finland has responded by placing volunteer troops at its disposal. Finnish troops have served under the UN flag in the Middle East (Suez, Sinai, Golan, Lebanon), former Yugoslavia, Cyprus and Africa (Namibia). The UN has also sent Finnish military observers to Somalia, Kuwait, Iraq, Kashmir and Afghanistan. Relative to its population, Finland has contributed more soldiers than any other member state, over 30 000 volunteers.

Finland has twice been elected to the UN Security Council (1969–70 and 1989–90), and several times to its Economic and Social Council and other agencies. The Under-General Secretary for Administrative Affairs and the General Secretary of the International Telecom-munications Union (ITU) were both Finns. The former, Martti Ahtisaari, was elected president of Finland in 1994. In close conjunction with the other Nordic countries, Finland ensures that at least one Nordic country is always represented on most UN bodies. In the General Assembly and major UN conferences the Nordic countries usually agree that one of them will speak on behalf of the others.

Many have been the speeches and statements concerning Finland's UN policy, but the most prestigious have often been made by the nation's presidents. In 1961 President Kekkonen stated that Finland saw its UN role more as a doctor than a judge, that it did not wish to deepen conflict and distrust between nations by condemning the behaviour of others, but rather to reduce tension and seek compromises. Nevertheless, Finland has actively condemned and opposed the use of violence, racial discrimination and other violations of human rights. One of the recognised prin-ciples of Finland's UN policy is that the organisation should be as representative as possible; thus it has strongly opposed the expulsion of member states.

# SECURITY AND DEFENCE POLICY

The aim of Finland's security policy is the preservation of the country's independence and the protection of its citizens. By her own actions she tries to prevent situations arising that might threaten the country's security.

Finland's security is based on its foreign policy, and supported by a defence system led by armed forces commensurate to the resources of the nation. The most important civil branches of defence are economic and civil defence, and military intelligence.

The 1974 Defence Act states that the main duties of the armed forces are:

– To control the nation's land, sea and air space, and ensure its territorial inviolability.
– The armed defence of the nation.
– To maintain and improve the country's defence preparedness, and provide the military training necessary for this purpose.
– To organise peacekeeping forces for possible deployment by the United Nations.

Finland's location and nearby areas of strategic importance naturally affect the importance of her military defence. Finnish

**A soldier from the Lapp Brigade on winter manoeuvres.**

**Swedish-made Draken fighters of the Finnish airforce at Pirkkala airbase.**

territory is not in itself a cause or reason for war, as there are no nuclear weapons on its soil, nor foreign military advisors or bases. It is extremely unlikely that a war would be waged against Finland alone or nuclear weapons used against her. Finland is prepared to defend every inch of her territory, and to prevent its use for attacks on strategic areas beyond its borders. The goal is that the existence and preparedness of the nation's armed forces is sufficient to deter would-be aggressors. Due to Nordic military policies Finland's primary defence considerations are south Finland, Lapland and Finnish air space.

Both branches of security, foreign policy and defence, are under the leadership of the president, who is supreme commander of the defence forces. The Defence Council is the highest consultative body and advises the president on defence matters. The council is chaired by the prime minister, and its members are the five ministers most concerned with defence, the commander-in-chief of the defence forces and the chief of the General Staff. Although the council has no executive power, its members have power in their own respective fields.

The Ministry of Defence is the highest administrative authority in the field of defence. It is responsible for legislation, adminis-trative and fiscal matters relating to national defence. The ministry is the link between the armed forces and the government.

The commander-in-chief of the defence forces directs the military defence of the nation with the aid of the general staff. He is directly responsible to the president for such military matters as staff, training and operations.

The Border Guard Service under the Ministry of the Interior is organised along military lines, and works in close conjunction with the defence forces. If defence considerations so require, it may be temporarily incorporated into the defence forces.

According to Finnish law all male citizens between the ages of 17 and 60 are duty bound to defend their country. Conscription is normally between the ages of 18 and 21 and lasts for 240 days, or 285 days in the more technical branches. For service-men in the most demanding fields, nco's and reserve officers national service is 330 days. Every year some 30 000 men are called-up in two or three drafts.

After national service all men are placed on reserve until the age of 60. About 45 000 reservists report annually for refresher courses. Refresher courses concentrate on pre-paring whole combat units for action. The defence forces have at their disposal a reserve of some 700 000 fully-equipped men.

National defence is based on a regional defence system, designed to take advantage of the special circumstances of the country. Main emphasis in this highly flexible, nationwide system is on land forces. The command system, which remains in a constant state of readiness, consists of seven military areas divided into 23 military districts. During peacetime garrisons serve as both training camps and permanent bases ensuring overall defence preparedness, and can be reinforced by reserves if the need arises. A more widespread mobilisation can be effected through the military districts. During

peacetime the task of the navy and air force is to maintain and ensure territorial integrity, and to provide support for regional defence during a time of crisis.

Most equipment for the defence forces is of domestic manufacture. Over 40 % of all basic equipment and replacements are Finnish made, thus guaranteeing their suitability to the conditions of the country.

Defence expenditure accounts for about 5 % of the annual budget and around 1.5 % of gnp. Taking into account the special conditions prevailing in Finland, a broad consensus exists that its armed forces are in harmony with the strategic position of the Nordic area.

# THE ECONOMY

Finland after the second world war could still be considered a semi-industrialised nation as the majority of the population was still engaged in agriculture and forestry. As late as 1950 46 % of the labour force worked in primary production, and some 27 % each in industry and services. Incomes were relatively low, rationing was still in force, and exports were unbalanced. One result of the heavy bill for war reparations to the Soviet Union was that Finland was forced to industrialise quickly.

From 1950 to 1974 the real growth in gdp was rapid, averaging 5 % per annum, so already in the 1970s Finland could be considered a highly developed post-industrial country. Since 1975 the growth in gdp has slowed down somewhat, although in the boom years of the 1980s it again increased to almost 6 per cent. This ceased as Finland entered a recession at the beginning of the 1990s, the reasons for which were the excessive overheating of the economy towards the end of the preceding decade, central and local government and corporate indebtedness, immoderate expansion during the 1970s and 1980s in the public sector, a growing balance of payments' deficit, and the simultaneous collapse of trade with the Soviet Union. The economy went into decline at the beginning of the 1990s, unemployment increased and the Finn markka was removed from its ties to the ECU within the EMS and allowed to float, thereby effectively devaluing it by some 25 per cent.

Calculated at market prices, per capita gdp in Finland in 1990 was one of the highest in the world. As a result of rapid industrialisation, the standard of living had by international criteria reached a high level. However, because of high costs largely due to climatic conditions, the purchasing power of Finnish incomes is somewhat lower, yet still above average for Europe.

The population has rapidly urbanised, and the structure of both industry and foreign trade radically changed. The main features of Finnish economic life today are the internationalisation of its corporations and the production and utilisation of advanced technology. Nowadays, only 8.5 % of the labour force is engaged in primary production and 29.6 % in industry, whereas services account for 58.6 per cent. Although about 44 % of the labour force has only received a basic education, a similar

Finland's high-tech marine engineering industry is renowned for its special vessels and oil rigs. The picture shows one of Rauma-Repola Offshore's jack-up rigs.

Countless lakes and a long coastline not only lure **Finns to the water, but have given them an incomparable skill in boat building. Skimming over the waters in a Swan boat is a sure way of forgetting everyday worries.**

percentage has acquired vocational or professional training and some 12 % a university education.

Finnish economic life is based on private ownership and free enterprise. In certain branches, however, the state has a monopoly; either *de jure* as with the sale of wines and spirits (Alko), or *de facto* as with the railways (Valtionrautatiet), air traffic (Finnair), oil refining (Neste) and electricity (Imatran Voima). Most of these state companies have

the same legal status as private ones.

Municipal authorities are responsible for power and water, and often local transport services. The public sector's share of industrial production is about 16 %, almost a half of transportation and communications, but only about 1 % of trade and agriculture.

**FOREIGN TRADE**

Due to the limited size of the domestic market, foreign trade is of vital importance to the Finnish economy.

In the first half of the present century exports relied heavily on the forest industry, particularly the products of the wood and paper industries. During the

**A Finnish-made Valmet tractor in action drawing a silage harvester.**

fifties, the metal and engineering industries began massive exports to the Soviet Union. With the growing integration of trade in Western Europe, Finland, in order to safeguard its export markets, joined EFTA under the FINEFTA Agreement of 1961. Along with other neutral nations, Finland signed a special free-trade agreement with the expanding EEC in 1973. The EEA agreement between the EFTA and EC countries is an important intermediate step on the road to wider economic integration in Europe. Finland's application to the European Union was approved, and a treaty of accession was signed in Corfu in 1994. The "yeses" carried the day in a consultative referendum, and Finland will become a full member in 1995.

Participation in the process of integration in Europe led to a major diversification of exports, with significant increases in the shares of the metal, engineering, clothing, electronic and chemical industries. The share of traditional forest industry products fell to about 40 % of the total. Some 44 % of Finnish exports go to EU countries like Germany, France, Great Britain, the Benelux countries and Italy. Finland's leading trading partner outside the Community is Sweden, followed by the United States

This multi-purpose, microprocessor-operated machine is the latest aid to wood felling.

A Finnish paper-making machine at the Shotton Paper Mill in Scotland.

and Japan. Trade with Russia and the other CIS countries has declined during the 1990s; exports in 1991 accounted for about 5 % of the total, and imports, largely crude oil and other fuels, for about 8 per cent.

## AGRICULTURE AND FORESTRY

Finnish farmers have typically mixed agriculture with forestry. Smallholders working the fields during the summer and the forests during the winter. However, since the early fifties both branches have been heavily mechanised, thus freeing the labour urgently required by other branches of the economy. Between 1950 and the early 1990s, the number of people engaged in agriculture and forestry has fallen from 46 to 8.5 per cent.

As increasing difficulties were experienced with the export of surplus produce it became necessary to cut back production, so there has been little real growth since the 1960s. The overall area under cultivation has diminished and the number of farms declined at the same time as their size has increased. Dairy farming accounts for about two thirds of total farm income and in 1991 there were about 450 000 dairy cattle in the country. Farms have specialised in dairy and beef cattle, pigs and chickens. The main exports are of meat, eggs and dairy products, of which Finnish Emmental cheese has made quite a name for itself. South Finland is the main area for arable cultivation, with a number of holdings specialising in market gardening and fur farming. Organic farming is unable to meet the growing demand from abroad. Of the country's 2.5 million hectares under cultivation some 0.6 million hectares is grassland, after which the most important crops are barley, oats, wheat, oleiferous plants, potatoes, s ugar beet and rye. Lapland is considered the land of dairy cattle and the herding of some 300 000 head of reindeer.

About 70 % of Finland is covered by forests. The total stock of growing trees is over 1660 million $m^3$, with a yearly felling rate in recent times slightly under the annual increase of almost 70 million $m^3$. The forests are being threatened by acid rain, due largely to industrial pollution from other countries. The main species of tree are pine (40 % of the yearly growth), spruce (37 %) and birch, followed by significant numbers of aspen and alder. Felled wood is used either as roundwood in the sawmill, plywood and board industries, or as fibre in the pulp and paper industries. Apart from industrial waste wood, the use of wood as a fuel has diminished considerably. Reforestation and the draining of wetlands increased considerably during the 1960s and 1970s. As a result of

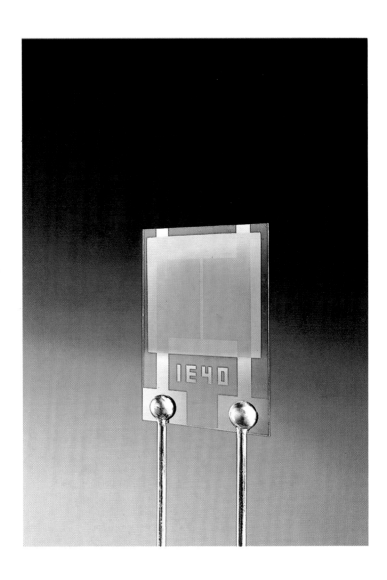

Above: Vaisala develops and
manufactures measuring instruments
for meteorological, environmental
and industrial use. The picture
shows a thin-film capacitive
humidity sensor.

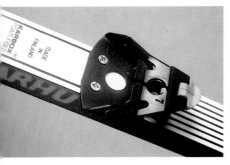

Examples of Finnish technology and industrial design. Above: Fiskars scissors, the most imitated Finnish product. Centre: helmet and ski binding. Below: Nokia's mobile telephone.

the restructuring of agriculture, an ever greater number of forests have passed into the hands of non-farming owners. Although the state owns about 24 % of the forests, its stake in the wood industry remains minimal.

**INDUSTRY**

During the inter-war years Finnish industry was characterised by a division into export-market oriented industry, represented by the wood industry, and home-market oriented industry. This division remained until the 1950s. War reparations had fully utilised the capacity of the metal and engineering industries, whereas other branches had been hampered by rationing. Once reparation payments had been completed in 1952 the Soviet Union Continued to place huge orders with the metal and engineering industries. As integration increased within Europe the wood and other industries began to receive orders from Western Europe.

Due to the country's massive forest resources and high-grade wood, exports from the pulp and paper industries still lead the field. In paper and cardboard exports, Finland is the second country in the world after Canada. About 80 % of the total production of the wood industry goes for export, accounting for almost 40 % of the total and 23 % of the value of industrially processed output. The share of high-grade paper and paper products within the industry is constantly increasing. The turnover of the industry's overseas subsidiaries accounts for over 15 % of the total.

Finland's most important branches of industry today are the metal and engineering industries, which account for about 30 % of total output and a similar percentage of total exports. Every third industrial worker is employed in these industries. There is little mining going on in Finland, yet the country is still an important producer of certain non-ferrous metals. The key branches in the metal industry are the high-tech production of steel and copper. The main products of the mechanical engineering industry are agricultural and forestry equipment, wood industry machines and equipment, fork trucks and lifts, consumer durables, electrical and electronic products. Finland is known throughout the world for its high-tech production of telephone exchanges, quality cars, mobile phones and consumer electronics (like TVs). The mechanical engineering industry also produces lorries and special sea-going vessels, such as icebreakers (Finland was once the leading manufacturer), luxury liners, leisure-time submarines, and oil rigs often specially designed for operation under extreme climatic

In this promised age of cheap imports, Finland's textile industry struggles to maintain its market position through quality and design. Its greatest successes have been in leisure and sportswear.

conditions.

The chemical industry has also grown rapidly and now accounts for about 10 % of total industrial production. In addition to oil refining and fertilizers, this branch also has a significant output of techno-chemical and pharmaceutical products.

Thanks to successful design Finland has managed to acquire recognition abroad with such consumer products as clothing and footwear, furniture, utility and decorative glass, cutlery and jewellery. Due to high quality and competitive prices, the food, alcohol, tobacco and printing industries have landed considerable orders from abroad.

Domestic energy (mainly hydro-electric, wood industry waste and peat produced) accounts for only 30 % of total consumption. Finland is thus heavily dependent upon energy imports. The share of oil has declined. Nowadays about 22 % of total energy consumption is produced by the country's four nuclear power stations, which account for about 40 % of electricity production.

**CONSTRUCTION**

As a result of migration, urbanisation and other social changes in the 1960s and 1970s, there was a major extension of the road, rail, harbour, canal and electricity networks, nuclear power stations were built, and a massive housing programme introduced. To keep pace with industrial development many new factories, offices and public buildings were constructed. In the 1990s, however, investments have concentrated on refurbishing and maintenance. The share of the construction industry in gdp was 9 % at the beginning of the 1970s, with annual housing production in the region of 70 000 units. During the following decade housing production fell to about 30 000–40 000 units a year, which forced building companies to seek contracts abroad.

**DOMESTIC TRADE**

The share of trade in total gdp has fluctuated between 10–11 % and 13–15 % of employment. Productivity has increased as a result of rationalisation, self-service and improved storage and distribution facilities. About 75 % of all food stores operate along self-service lines. Rapid urbanisation and increased car ownership have contributed to the demise of small shops in the more distant areas and their replacement by downtown multi-store shopping malls, department stores and supermarkets. Two thirds of private consumption is channeled through the retail trade organised into a number of competing chains. Although fierce competition exists in the wholesale and retail trade in everyday goods, the recession has done much to induce the groups to cooperate. The state-owned Alko has a monopoly of the sale of wines, spirits and strong beers, though food shops are allowed to sell low-alcohol beers.

## TRANSPORT AND COMMUNICATIONS

Finland's geographical location, dispersed population and highly variable climate set heavy technical and economic strains on transportation. The share of transport in both gdp and employment varies from 7–9 per cent.

Icebreakers ensure that the main harbours are kept open for shipping even during severe winters. The Saimaa Canal offers access from the Baltic to the east Finnish lake district for suitably-sized vessels. Otherwise traffic on the inland waterways, and to an increasing extent also log floating, has been replaced by road transport. Most of Finland's merchant navy consists of luxury ferries for carrying passengers and freight, and highly automatised container and bulk cargo carriers.

Most of the country's approximately 75 000 km road network has been properly surfaced. An efficient fleet of snow ploughs keep the roads open during winter. The normal speed limits are 120 or 100 km/h on the motorways, 100 or 80 km/h on main roads, 80 km/h on subsidiary roads, and 50 km/h in built-up areas. During winter the speed limit is lowered on main roads to minimise accidents and prevent excessive wear-and-tear as studded tyres are not only permitted but are compulsory in wintertime. The driving test also requires experience on slippery roads. There are some 2.2 million road vehicles in Finland, almost 90 % of them private cars. Together they constitute a serious threat to the railways. Of the 6 000 km of track in Finland, the most important sections (about 25 % of the total) have been electrified, the rest use diesel engines. All major towns operate their own local transport systems. Helsinki's, for instance, includes buses, trams, suburban trains and a metro.

The domestic airline network is one of the best in Europe. The state-owned Finnair flies to all the major industrial countries, the longest hauls being to Japan and the United States.

For all intents and purposes, automatic telecommunications cover the whole country. With almost 60 out of every 100 inhabitants on the phone and a mobile phone penetration of almost 10 %, Finland is near the top of the world league. Its telephone network and other communi-cation systems are, internatio-nally speaking, top grade. About half of the long-distance network has been digitalised and the isdn network

**A young finance expert hurries to the stock market.**

now being installed will greatly improve computer communications. The number of people working with information technology is quite considerable and i n the Helsinki metropolitan area it is almost half.

### BANKING AND INSURANCE

The money market is regulated by the central bank, the Bank of Finland (established in 1811), by means of bank and discount rates and currency regulations. The Bank's operations are in turn supervised by parliament. The national currency is the *markka,*

the Finnish mark (FIM), which is divided into 100 *penni.* The mark was unilaterally tied to the ECU within the EMS, but speculation on the international currency market and the economic recession forced the Bank of Finland to change its policy. Since 1992 the Finnish mark has floated in much the same way as the pound sterling, the Swedish and Norwegian crowns and several other European currencies.

There are three main banking groups: private commercial banks (46 % of all deposits), co-operative banks (27 %) and savings banks (26 %). In respect to the services offered these are becoming increasingly similar to each other. The use of bank and

Ever more Finns acquire a weekend or summer cottage in the countryside in addition to their town dwelling. Shares in Lapp skiing centres or holiday condominiums in the sunny south are also popular.

credit cards has become widespread. A major restructuring of banking is underway, with small banks being merged, branches closed to improve profitability, and savings banks being converted into limited companies. The Government Guarantee Fund has introduced plans for entirely new forms of banking. Business on the Helsinki Stock Exchange is managed through private and bank brokers. Foreign investors have shown an interest in listed companies, because of the extremely stable political conditions prevailing in the country. In addition to the banks and other financial institutions, the other important sources of loans are the state and insurance companies. Although there are a considerable number of insurance companies, most business is concentrated in the ten largest. The most profitable lines of business are the compulsory pension scheme and other obligatory insurances.

**THE PUBLIC SECTOR**

The growth in overall production and services is due to the extension of publicly-financed activities. The civil service, defence, education and research, hospital and health services, and social security are an integral part of Finnish society. There are considerably more people working in the services than in industry.

Public services are maintained out of taxation by either the state or the local municipalities. The state aids municipalities in proportion to their incomes.

The most important direct tax is that levied by local authorities on all residents, the rate being under 20 % of their incomes. State income tax is progressive, and at most the rate is slightly under 40 % of taxable income. The rates for the state income and property taxes, as well as the local tax, are determined annually.

The main indirect tax is VAT, the rate of which, with certain exceptions, is 22 % on the retail price. Excise taxes are imposed on fuels, tobacco and alcoholic beverages. The motor vehicle tax is one of the highest in the world. Stamp duty is another important source of income for the state. The importance of customs duties, has radically declined.

The state's share of direct taxation is about 60 %, the local authorities 25 %, and the remaining 14 % consists largely of social security contributions. The trend in tax policy has been towards indirect taxation. Different forms of income transfers and benefits to individuals and companies alike play an important part in the public economy. In addition to public housing programmes, various interest-subsidised loans account for a major part of both central and local government

# 1993

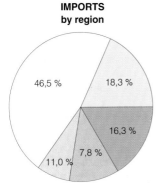

**IMPORTS**
**by region**

EC  46,5 %
EFTA  18,3 %
Other Europe 11,0 %
Developing countries 7,8 %
Other countries 16,3 %

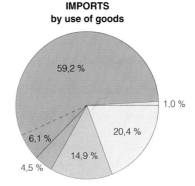

**IMPORTS**
**by use of goods**

Raw materials 59,2 %
Crude oil 6,1 %
Fuels 4,5 %
Investment goods 14,9 %
Consumer goods 20,4 %
Other articles 1,0 %

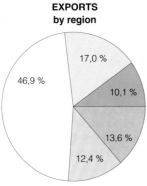

**EXPORTS**
**by region**

EC 46,9 %
EFTA 17,0 %
Other Europe 10,1 %
Other countries 13,6 %
Developing countries 12,4 %

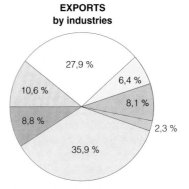

**EXPORTS**
**by industries**

Paper and graphic industry 27,9 %
Chemical industry 10,6 %
Basic metal industry 8,8 %
Metal product and machine industry 35,9 %
Textile, clothing and leather industry 2,3 %
Wood industry 8,1 %
Other industries 6,4 %

expenditure. The largest items of state and municipal expenses are for education, cultural activities and social security.

## CONSUMPTION AND THE STANDARD OF LIVING

The share of food in private consumption is about 20 %, with alcohol and tobacco accounting for over 3 per cent. The average size of dwellings is approximately 70 m$^2$ and the space per inhabitant is about 26–27 m$^2$. Thanks to a socially-oriented housing programme few people any more have to endure cramped living conditions. Nowadays over 60 % of the people own their own homes and some 20 % live in council houses. There are, in addition, some 300 000 leisure-time second homes. Housing absorbs about 17 % of household income. Finnish homes are well-upholstered and saturation point has been reached with many household appliances. The main fields of expansion in private consumption are transportation (cars), electronics, recreation and hobbies, travel, culture and education, which together account for about 40 %.

Finnish consumer protection law establishes the general principles governing the sale and marketing of goods and services, and regulates the relationship between buyers and sellers. A special board exists to handle without charge consumer complaints concerning the sale and marketing of consumer goods. The sale and marketing of real estate and apartments is also regulated by law. Another law determines responsibility for products and regulates the relationship between the consumer and the manufacturer and seller of the goods.

The public sector in Finland also provides free basic education, excellent further educational facilities, a virtually free national health service, extensive social security, subsidised public transport and cultural amenities.

## BALANCING THE NATIONAL ECONOMY

Difficulties have been experienced during the 1990s with balancing the national economy. Of the total labour force of some 2.5 million people, almost 500 000 have been unemployed during the early 1990s. Even so, among certain skilled branches, there remains a shortage of labour. The 6–10 % annual rise in the cost of living is partly due to global cyclical factors. The balance of payments has long been in debt, but the growth in exports has narrowed the gap. One of the main problems in balancing the budget is the unexpected fall in government tax revenue due to the recession.

# SOCIAL SECURITY

After decades of steady progress, Finland's system of social security is now one of the finest in the world. No less than 18.5 % of the budget goes on social expenditure.

The system covers all potential social risks, and its most important aspect is social insurance. This includes national and employment pension schemes, accident and health insurance, and unemployment assistance and benefits. Support services for families, the elderly and handicapped continue to be in great demand.

## HEALTH INSURANCE

The health insurance scheme administered by the National Pensions Institution covers all people residing in Finland, offering them medical attention, laboratory and x-ray examination, and even physiotherapy for a nominal fee. Patients are required to pay part of the cost of pre-scribed medicines, except in cases of the chronically sick

**Rehabilitation is of primary importance in health care. This is a kinetic measuring apparatus for assessing the straightening abilities of patients suffering from chronic back trouble. The results are used in planning physiotherapy programmes.**

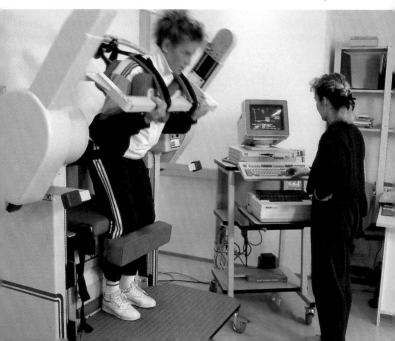

when they are free.

A small charge, roughly equivalent to running costs, is levied on hospital treatment. All health and hospital expenses, as well as necessary travel expenses, over a certain minimum sum are refunded.

Part of the cost of private medical attention and examination is also covered. All those born in 1956 and after are included within the dental treatment scheme, likewise war veterans. All those of working age receive a daily allowance amounting to 80 % of their salary when ill. And for those not actually in employment, a minimum daily allowance is paid.

A maternity allowance is paid on the same basis as the daily sickness allowance. This is paid for a period of ten months, part of which is parental leave when either the mother or father can look after their baby. The allowance is paid even if the mother returns to work prior to the end of her maternity leave.

**PENSION INSURANCE**

The normal pensionable age in Finland for both men and women is 65 years, although in many occupations it is lower. Upon reaching pensionable age, everybody receives the national pension in addition to an employment pension if they have been working. The object of the latter is to ensure continuance of the same standard of living enjoyed whilst working.

The national pension is paid to all living in Finland irrespective of their previous earnings. The amount paid depends on the wealth and income of the individual.

The amount of the employment pension is directly related to previous earnings and the number of years worked. The maximum employment pension, 60 % of salary, is paid after 40 years in work. The larger the employment pension, the smaller the national pension. No upper limit is set on pensions in Finland.

Central and local authority employees, and those working in other public bodies, have their own pension schemes that are very similar to the employment pension scheme.

**UNEMPLOYMENT ASSISTANCE**

Nearly all organised workers belong to voluntary unemployment benefit funds operated by the trade unions. In order to draw unemployment benefit from the fund a worker must have been a member for at least six months. A ceiling is set to the annual benefits paid and to those paid over a three-year period. The funds are financed by the employers, the state, and less importantly the members.

The unemployment benefit paid by the state to those not covered by the funds is roughly propor-tionate to those in a comparable occupation. It is

**There are several rehabilitation institutes for disabled war veterans. Seated volley ball has been developed especially for amputee patients.**

only enough to cover very basic needs.

### ACCIDENT INSURANCE

Employers are compelled by law to insure their employees against loss of earnings and medical costs incurred as a result of accidents at work or occupational diseases. Third party motor insurance is compulsory for all motor vehicle owners.

### FAMILY ALLOWANCES

Child benefit is paid to the parents of all children under 17 residing in Finland. An increased benefit is paid on children under the age of three. Municipalities operate day-care centres for the pre-school aged children of working parents. About one third of all children are looked after in the homes of local-authority supervised and approved child minders. Families with an under three-year-old child, managed at home or by a private child minder, are paid a monthly allowance. There is considerable variation in the provision of day-care centre facilities by local authorities, but they are required by law to provide places for all under three-year-old children in need. There are still not enough municipal day-care places for all children under school age.

Families with a handicapped or seriously ill child under 16 are

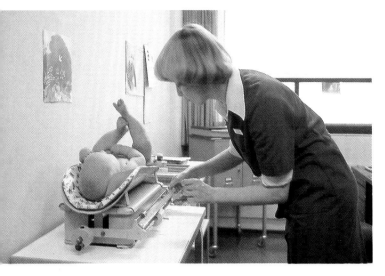

**A baby on its' regular check-up visit to the clinic.**

entitled to home-care assistance. A mother, whose child does not receive financial assistance from the father, receives a state maintenance benefit.

All expectant mothers receive a maternity gift: either a parcel of baby clothes and materials or money, the former being worth more than the latter.

### CARE OF THE ELDERLY

Municipalities arrange many different services, at a nominal charge, to help elderly people with such everyday chores as cleaning, cooking, shopping, running errands and trans- portation. Then there are special centres where senior citizens can obtain information and meet people. Some of these function in conjunction with old people's homes. Institutional care is provided for some 6 % of all those over 65 years of age. Apartment blocks have also been built for the elderly which take into account their special needs. Similar places have been built for the handicapped.

## HEALTH CARE

### HEALTH CENTRES

Local authorities, either alone or together with neighbouring areas, are required under the national health service to maintain health centres.

Their function is to provide the local population with medical services, first aid, antenatal and postnatal clinical services, and the school health care service. Most centres have four GPs, a

Families with children have a right to daycare, and since 1990 this has been realised for those with under three-year-olds.

**Town and municipal sanitation services keep the roads clean and free from snow.**

midwife, and a staff of nurses and others. One of their most important tasks is to give advice and check the health of expectant and nursing mothers, and regularly check the health of the children from the time they are born to when they go to school. So effective is this system that Finland has an extremely low level of child mortality. Virtually all children attend the clinics for regular medical checks, innoculations, etc, the details of which are entered in their health cards, which accompany them through-out school. Health centres are also responsible for organising the local ambulance service.

Although health centres provide the basic medical services required, there are also private centres where authorised doctors practice medicine, often in addition to their hospital duties.

### HOSPITALS

In many health centres there are also wards, but these are mainly intended for chronic patients. The centre's function is to decide whether a patient should go for hospital treatment or examination by a specialist. The country is divided into 21 hospital districts, and the muncipalities within the district are responsible for the maintenance of their central hospital. The state contributes towards the cost in proportion to the means of the district in question.

Central hospitals must provide

wards for the treatment of most general diseases. Doctors, though not interns, must be specialists. Five of the central hospitals are university teaching hospitals.

Smaller local units supplement the services of the district central hospitals, and are required to provide treatment in three specialist fields. They are also maintained by the local authorities, but there is no nationwide system as they are established on a voluntary basis.

In addition to the central and local hospitals, there are mental institutions, military and penal hospitals, etc. The maintenance of hospital services has been traditionally thought of as a charge on the community, so there are few private ones. There are some 430 hospitals in Finland, providing 13 beds per thousand inhabitants.

## PATIENTS

Patients are hospitalised only on the recommendation of a health centre GP, except in the case of accidents and emergencies. In this way the most intensive use is made of hospital resources. Patients are normally admitted to their local hospital.

## ENVIRONMENTAL HEALTH

Environmental health is the responsibility of the local authorities, and involves environmental hygiene, control of foodstuffs and poisons, occupational health and veterinary medicine.

Great stress is placed upon food hygiene and safety: control of the production, storage and sale of food, and supervising the health of those handling food. Environmental health also covers drinking water, clean air and noise control. A nationwide system has been introduced for the disposal of problem wastes.

## HOUSING POLICY

Housing production clearly reflects the rapid urbanisation of Finland that has taken place since the early 1950s. So great was the pressure that over half of existing housing was built during the last twentyfive years.

The goal of development area policy is to balance out regional inequalities and stem the flow of rural people to the southern conurbations. To achieve this employment, living standards and basic services are guaranteed in these areas.

Local authorities are responsible for the overall living environment. All building is in accordance with an approved local plan, subject to the availability of capital and land ownership relations. Residents' associations and private citizens have shown a growing interest in communal planning, due to the increased importance of the quality of life. By improving the level of their surroundings they also improve the quality of their houses and apartments.

Rentable dwellings account for over 20 % of the total. The state grants long-term, low-interest loans with which less well-off people can buy or build their own homes. These loans are for 15–20 years.

Families with children, old people and students can obtain a housing allowance to help them maintain a reasonable standard of living. Living costs in Finland are quite high, largely due to the need to build to withstand arctic conditions, but also because of strict safety regulations.

The law on consumer protection also applies to the sale and marketing of houses and flats.

### LABOUR POLICY

Labour policy concerns employer-employee relations, work safety and manpower questions. Employers and employees are required to co-operate to maintain and develop work safety. Special work safety committees exist in larger companies with representatives appointed by both sides. These either carry out their own safety inspections, or participate in

those made by the state or local authorities.

Work safety regulations cover such matters as work place lighting, temperature, noise levels and ventilation, safety devices on machinery, civil defence equipment, advice and instructions, and organising first aid.

Although the 8 hour day, 40 hour week is normal, many work less, as for example 36 hours in a regular three-shift working week. Parents with babies or children in their first year at school have the possibility of working shorter hours. Employees are entitled to a minimum of 2 days holiday for each month worked; some have more and also a week-long winter holiday. The content of employment contracts between employers and employees is regulated by law. Collective bargaining agreements between the employers' confederations and the trade unions prescribe wage and salary levels, social benefits, period of notice, etc. General agreements on wages and salaries are mostly negotiated annually.

**Over half of the total number of houses in Finland were built in the last twentyfive years. The aerial view is from a western suburb of Espoo in the greater metropolitan area of Helsinki.**

# THE CHURCH

Almost exactly 90 % of Finns belong to the Evangelical Lutheran Church, and another 3 % to registered or unregistered denominations.

Although Christianity had probably reached Finland by the end of the first millennium AD, it was not until the 12th century that the Roman Catholic Church became established. This followed the so-called crusade of the Swedish king Eric and his English-born bishop Henry to south-west Finland. The influence of the Orthodox Church spread into the country from the east, gathering under its wing all those who lived in what is now east Karelia. Thus religious and cultural boundaries deepened the country's division into two spheres of influence: Novgorod and Russia on the one side and Swedish Finland on the other.

Following the Reformation in Scandinavia and Finland in the 16th century, Finland became Lutheran. Complete freedom of religion, however, was not guaranteed until 1923. Nowadays there are about 600 Lutheran parishes in the country with over 4.3 million members

**Many of Finland's beautiful old wooden churches have survived. The one in the picture is in Vimpeli.**

(85,9 % of the population), making it the world's third largest Lutheran church.

The clearly secular character of Finnish society owes much to the strong element of individualism in Protestantism. Nevertheless, the great majority of Finns still value the church and its works, and use it at the main junctures of their lives. Over 90 % of all children are baptised and confirmed. Only a few adult members prefer to be married in a registry office, and many non-members desire a church funeral. Religious programmes on the radio and TV are very popular.

The church most easily reaches children, youth and the elderly. It also offers family guidance and distress phone services.

Parishes have a wide degree of financial and operational independence, electing their own priests and parish officials. The administrative bodies are elected every four years.

The 600 parishes are divided into eight dioceses, one of which is Swedish-speaking, each with its own bishop and chapter. Bishops are appointed by the president from a short list of three proposed by the chapter. Turku, the capital of Finland until 1812, is still the seat of the archbishop, though the National Ecclesiastical Board, which manages the administration and

**Women have been ordained in Finland since 1988. The picture shows the youth curate of Tuusula at a confirmation class camp.**

finances of the church, is in Helsinki.

The highest decision-making body is the Church Assembly or Synod, one-third of whose members are clergy and two-thirds laity. Its tasks include deciding upon church operations and finances, approving ecclesiastical books and entering into agreements with other churches. Another important function is pro-posing amendments to the Ecclesiastical Act which must then go to parliament for approval. Parliament can either accept or reject them, but not change them, and in practice always approves them. After a heated debate the assembly finally accepted the ordination of women in 1986, and two years later parliament gave its assent to the proposed amendment to the Ecclesiatical Act. The same year the first female theological graduates were ordained, thus enabling them to perform all church duties. The office of bishop is also now open to women.

Over the last century the bond between church and state has so weakened that the former is nowadays virtually independent of the latter. One important link remains: parishes have the right

**Interior of the church of Valamo monastery in Heinävesi.**

to levy taxes. This is collected by the inland revenue office along with other income taxes. Non-members of the Evangelical Lutheran and Orthodox churches do not pay church tax, though companies must. This is considered as payment for such church-provided communal services as the maintenance of the local registers of births, deaths and marriages for church members and the upkeep of graveyards.

Children receive or are excused from religious instruction at school in accordance with their parents' beliefs.

With a membership of almost 60 000, the Orthodox Church is the second largest church in Finland. Its earlier centres are in those parts of Karelia now in Russia. For long the church suffered from the dispersion of its congregation throughout the country as a result of the war, but nowadays it is again thriving and vigorous. Its importance in Finland is far greater than its modest membership presupposes.

After the two main churches, the most significant religious group in Finland, at least in respect to the activity of its members, is the Pentecostal movement. As its congregations are not registered, it is estimated to have some 50 000 members. The other groups are much smaller and include some 4000 Roman Catholics, 12 500 members of the Finnish Free Church, 5000 Adventists, etc. The Jewish community has more than a thousand members, the Islamic community slightly less, and there are about 13 000 Jehovah's Witnesses.

# SCHOOLS AND EDUCATION

Compulsory schooling takes place in Finland between the ages of 7 and 16, and there is additional provision for voluntary education for pre-school children. Basic education is given to all children upon reaching the age of seven in comprehensive schools consisting of nine compulsory forms and an optional tenth. Further education is voluntary, either in the three-year upper secondary schools or 2–5-year courses in vocational schools. Higher education is provided by the universities.

Education, science and culture account for 17–18 % of total government expenditure.

### PRE-SCHOOL EDUCATION

It is the task of the Ministry for Social Affairs and Health and the local authorities to arrange day care for the under seven-year-old children of working parents. This is organised either in municipal day-care centres or in the homes of approved childminders. The latter cope with about one third of total demand. As over three quarters of the mothers of under school-age children go to work, there is a desperate shortage of places in municipal day-care centres, especially in the larger towns.

Another function of day care is to augment home upbringing and ensure the balanced development of a child's personality.

Applicants for day-care centre teacher training are required to have matriculated. The course lasts three years, sufficient time

**Organised hobbies are a feature of kindergarden life. These young actors are king and queen in the school play.**

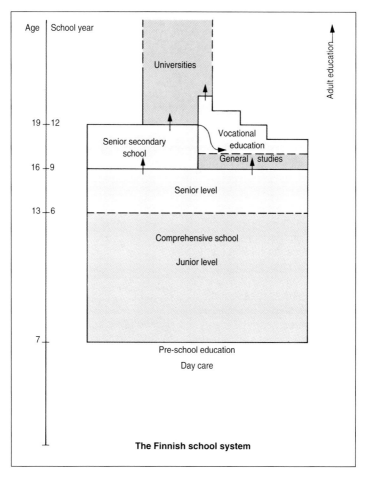

**The Finnish school system**

to provide potential teachers with a thorough theoretical background.

**COMPREHENSIVE SCHOOLS**

The aim of comprehensives is to provide a socio-ethical and aesthetic education in addition to the traditional subjects. Thus a good memory is no longer so important as the ability to study and think, and develop one's personality.

Although a comprehensive school may have a pre-school form for 6-year-old children, it is normally divided into two parts. At the junior level (forms 1–6) all children receive exactly the same education, given by their form teachers except in the case of languages. At the senior level

| | Monday | Tuesday | Wednesday | Thursday | Friday |
|---|---|---|---|---|---|
| 9–10 | Geography | Finnish | Rk | Finnish | Maths |
| 10–11 | Maths | Finnish | Geography | Geography | Finnish |
| 11–12 | Art | Music | Maths | Finnish | Civics |
| 12–13 | Art | Maths | History | English | Handicrafts |
| 13–14 | Pe | English | Pe | Pe | Handicrafts |
| 14–15 | | History | | | |

**6th class comrehensive school timetable**

(forms 7–9) teachers teach their own subjects. The junior level week is between 20 and 26 hours, and the senior level 30 hours.

The comprehensive aims at providing children with a general education. Compulsory subjects at the junior level are mathematics, religious knowledge, environmental studies, Finnish or Swedish (depending on the child's mother tongue), foreign languages (mostly English), history and social studies, civics, biology and geography, physical education, music, art and handicrafts.

The same subjects are also taught at the senior level with the exception of environmental studies. New compulsory subjects are chemistry and physics, home economics, and the second official language. Senior level pupils can also take such optional extras as economics, other foreign languages, agriculture or computer studies.

By international standards Finns place great emphasis on studying foreign languages – work on the first one starts in the third form – but rather less on their mother tongue and mathematics. Pupils also receive study and career guidance, as well as regular extra tuition and counselling if required.

As parts of Finland are very sparsely populated, rural schools are small, with only two or three teachers, and have joint forms in which the age difference may be as great as four years. An effort is being made to apply the teaching advantage of small forms to the towns, and also to decentralise decision making in respect to the organisation of teaching.

Training for comprehensive school form teachers is given in the universities, and there are seven Finnish-language and one Swedish-language faculties, each with its own demonstration school. The course lasts 4–5 years, and for junior and senior level subject teachers 5–6 years.

The leading publishers offer a wide choice of textbooks. Comprehensive school textbooks are chosen by the local board of

**The Heureka Science Centre in Vantaa is a favourite among comprehensive school children. Here they are studying the movement of a chaotic pendulum.**

education on the recommendation of the teachers.

The municipality is responsible for arranging general education. Tuition, materials and school meals are all free, and if the journey to school is over 5 km then there is free transportation. Local authorities receive aid from the state to maintain schools in accordance with their means. This can be as high as 100 %.

**SENIOR SECONDARY EDUCATION**
There are two types of senior secondary education in Finland: the three-year senior secondary school, *lukio*, similar to the British sixth form, which represents the traditional academic line, and the vocational schools. One of the problems with the present system of vocational education

Some of them are compulsory, others optional. Careers counselling is also given. There are special *lukios* for those with a special talent for music, art or physical education.

Nowadays, most senior secondary schools are run by the muncipality, and only a few by the state or privately.

At the end of the three years, the knowledge and abilities of pupils are tested in the nationwide "student exam" or matriculation held in spring and autumn. Matriculation is the basic requirement for a higher education, and every year there are some 30 000 new students. As there are only 18 000 university places each year, some of which are reserved, many of these newly-qualified students must seek a vocational education or go to work.

In vocational education, pupils choose a basic line from 25 different trades and professions. Each of these is divided into two stages, a general and specialised phase. The year-long general phase has the same content for all pupils, after which they specialise in their specific trade. These specialised courses vary in level and last from one to four years. For example, in car mechanics a pupil can qualify as a skilled fitter after the short course, a technician after the middle course, and an engineer after the longest course. There are 240 lines varying in content

is its fragmentation into many different lines of study.

Senior secondary education is now based on modules or courses, each one lasting 38 study hours. There may be several courses in the same subject before the final examination. Pupils study the following subjects: Finnish and Swedish, 1–3 foreign languages, mathematics, physics, chemistry, geography, biology, psychology, reglious knowledge, art or music, physical education and hygiene.

White-capped students celebrate the official first day of spring (May 1st) with songs, champagne and balloons.

The 350th anniversary of Helsinki University was celebrated in 1990 with no less than five degree conferment ceremonies. Here the procession moves from the university building to Helsinki Cathedral.

and level to choose from, plus a dozen or so special study lines.

All those who have completed the longest specialised courses are entitled to continue their education at a university.

Pupils undergoing upper secondary education can apply for non-returnable study grants.

About half of the vocational schools are run by the municipalities, a third by the state and the rest privately. The state, however, covers between 70 and 100 % of all their expenses.

## HIGHER EDUCATION

Finland's first university, the Royal Academy of Turku, was founded in 1640 when the country was part of Sweden, and transferred to Helsinki in 1828 when that town became the new capital. In 1990 it thus celebrated its 350th anniversary. Prior to independence two other institutions of higher education, one technical and one commercial, were established, and immediately afterwards two new universities.

With the aim of regional equality in mind, several other universities have been established since the 1950s. Nowadays there are 17 universities and three art academies, with a total student population of 80 000. The largest is the University of Helsinki (about

26 000 students), then come the universities of Turku and Tampere (each with almost 10 000 students), the University of Technology in Espoo, near Helsinki (over 9000 students), Oulu University (over 8000 students) and Jyväskylä University (about 7000 students).

Each year the universities take about 18 000 new students, some of whom come up from the vocational schools. The number trying to get in greatly exceeds the number of places, often many times over. The basic criteria for entrance are the senior secondary (or vocational) school leaving report, matriculation grades and success in the entrance exams. Over half of the undergraduates are women.

The universities are directly under the Ministry of Education and state owned. They are, however, self-governing, and the administrative bodies of some have representatives not only of the professors, but also the other teachers, staff, and even the students.

Students may apply for state grants or state-guaranteed loans from the banks to finance their education. Via the students' unions, the state also subsidises student hostels, health care and meals.

An effort has been made to closely relate scientific education to professional occupations. The number of study weeks required for a degree is the best indication of the breadth of study. A study week means 40 hours of independent study. In most fields students must first obtain a basic (Bachelor's or Master's) degree in general, specific and in-depth studies. This usually requires 160 study weeks or 4–5 years of study. After the first degree students can go on, straight away if they wish, to study for their Licenciate or PhD.

The number of students in the arts and social sciences has been deliberately reduced in favour of the natural sciences, technology and medicine. As teaching and research are closely related, this change is also clearly reflected in research. The scientific level of research is the responsibility of the professors. The number of professors is divided between the disciplines as follows: arts and social sciences 36 %, natural sciences 28 %, technology 18 % and medicine 18 %.

Higher education is open to all at the numerous summer universities held every year. Only part of the tuition is at university

**An exacting entrance examination must be passed before being admitted to university, and only about 35 % make it. The picture is of the university library, in Senate Square, Helsinki, and considered to be the most beautiful work of the architect Carl Ludvig Engel.**

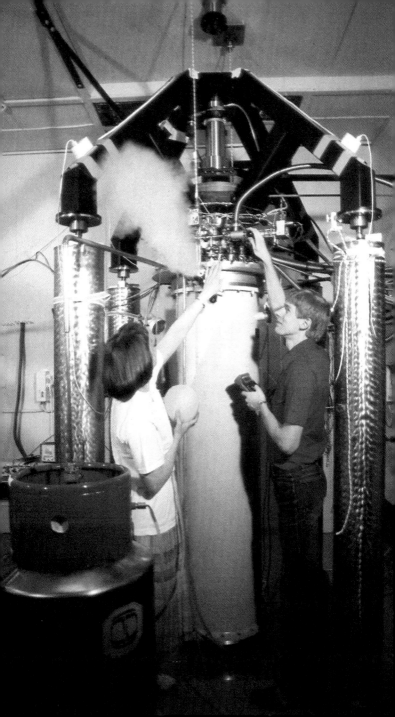

level, the rest is to supplement vocational or upper secondary education.

**RESEARCH**
Research accounts for about 2.3 % of the national budget, and almost a fifth of this goes to TEKES, the Centre for Technology Development. As a percentage of gnp, public and private sector expenditure on R&D is almost 2 %. Over half of this comes from private sources. Although industry operates its own research institutes, it also finances university research programmes, particularly technological research which absorbs over half of the available funds.

Public sector research funds are used to finance university research and the work of the 25 ministry-run research institutes. Of this about a quarter goes to the universities, which accounts for about 70 % of their expenditure on research. Some

60 % of university research work is primary, 30 % applied, and 10 % development in which industry also participates. About 85 % of the country's scientific literature is in the university libraries.

The administration of scientific work is centred in the Academy of Finland under the Ministry of Education. It is divided into seven councils representing the different branches of science. It finances research projects, normally for set periods. Most of the researchers work in the universities, who receive about a tenth of their research budget from the Academy. The Academy is also responsible for scientific policy making.

Historical and folklore research in Finland has been of major national importance, and one field of continued interest is that of the Finno-Ugrian languages. Philosophical research has been the most successful internationally. Also work in the social sciences has widened during the last three decades.

Research traditions are of great importance in a small country. In mathemathics, for example, one can talk of the Finnish school of function theory. Mathematics, unlike the natural sciences, does not demand huge investments, nevertheless research in the latter is at an international level. Likewise medical research, where notable work has been done into the use

**A cryostat constructed in the Low Temperature Laboratory of the Helsinki University of Technology. The aparatus is used for investigating the properties of rotating superfluid $^3$He. At low temperatures helium turns into a superfluid; the liquid has no viscosity and some vortices are created on the surface of the liquid. When experiments are made, the temperature of the inner parts of the cryostat is 1mK (about − 273.15°C).**

of interferon to combat cancer and virus infections. The North Karelia Project concerning the effect of life style on health (more specifically, the role of food in causing hypertension) has received international recognition.

Finland has also been a pioneer in agricultural and forestry research, especially in such fields as forest type theory and resource evaluation.

Part of the research work done in technology and engineering has been in collaboration with Finnish industry. International recognition has been given for work in the development of chrome steel, corrosion studies and copper flash-smelting processes.

The leading figures in Finnish research today include Georg Henrik von Wright, Jaakko Hintikka and Raimo Tuomela in philosophy and logic, Jaakko Paunio in economics, Erik Allardt in sociology, Olli Lehto in mathematics, Kari Cantell for his work on interferon, Olli Lounasmaa in physics and Martti Tiuri in communications.

**ADULT EDUCATION**

Alongside full-time education aimed at a degree or some other qualification, there exists a very diverse and informal system of voluntary adult education. Originally this was intended to provide both a general education and stimulate leisure-time activities, often in preparation for work in the community. However, during the 1980s increasing emphasis was placed on vocational training.

Adult education is arranged through different associations and organisations, and is partly state supported. Most of the courses are organised through a nationwide network of civic and workers' institutes, with more than 600 000 students. The first institutes were established in 1899, and most are maintained by the local authorities. Courses, mainly held in the evenings, are of a general educational, social or leisure-oriented nature. Some institutes offer upper secondary school courses for those going to work, but only in exceptional circumstances can examination certificates be given.

A general, social and vocational education is also provided in folk institutes (established in 1899) and folk academies. These are residential and take about 7000 students a year. Some of them are entitled to give upper secondary school leaving certificates.

Many political parties and trade unions have ideological and educational associations that arrange lectures, courses and seminars. They have also established numerous study centres to further their activities. Working methods vary, but perhaps the most popular are the study circles which embrace

**Although Toimela is a private adult educational institute it still receives state assistance. It teaches languages, mathematics, art, gymnastics and music. In the picture an art student at work.**

some 20 000 students each year.

There are also about 130 music schools with some 50 000 students, and 12 sports institutes, four of which produce physical education instructors.

Correspondence institutes offer both general and vocational education, the latter often organised by industry and business. Radio and TV courses are increasing and extremely popular.

Essential to adult education are the extensive lending facilities of the state-supported libraries, and the lectures, exhibitions and other cultural events which they arrange.

Employment courses for those facing unemployment or already unemployed, or in need of further training or retraining, are given in vocational course centres. With the rapid restructuring of industrial and business life, a growing number of people of working age need to attend retraining courses. These centres are maintained jointly by the educational and employment authorities. Instruction is free, travel and accommodation expenses and meals are paid for, and participants receive a daily allowance.

The open university is rapidly expanding, and the universities maintain supplementary educational centres to coordinate these activities. Because the country is so vast, auxiliary forms of education such as the telephone and computer are used. Multiform education is provided as 39 institutes, and some 30 000 students are enrolled in the open university.

Vocational education administered by the educational authorities reaches almost 300 000 adults each year. The number attending employment courses exceeds the OECD recommended level, that is more than 1 % of the labour force.

# CULTURE

The roots of Finnish culture lie deep in prehistory, in the customs and beliefs of the ancient Finns. These are most graphically portrayed in the national epic, the *Kalevala*, compiled by Elias Lönnrot from the oral memories of rune singers in the early 19th century.

Finland's cultural development has also been affected by its long association with Sweden and the Roman Catholic church, ancient trading links with Germany and the Baltic states, and the Eastern influence, seen most clearly in the role of the Orthodox church in Karelia. The spread of new cultural influences in the western areas was facilitated by more populous village settlements, whereas the scattered communities in Karelia favoured the retention of ancient traditions.

With only some 15 % of borrowed words in the language, this might attest to cultural continuity, but on closer analysis these words have come from all directions, from the Baltic, Sweden and Russia. The absorption of these influences over the centuries can be recognised in the multiple nuances of modern Finnish culture.

## FOLK TRADITIONS AND FESTIVALS

In folk tradition, the relationship of Finns to nature traces its origin back to pagan times, when they worshipped the many gods and spirits that personified nature and the elements. The greatest of these was *Ukko*, god of thunder and lightning, and his wife *Rauni*, mother nature, and who together took care of the weather and the seasons. He lives on in modern Finnish in the word for thunder, *ukkonen*. Ancient Finns were not particularly worried about these gods, for when trouble faced the tribe or family, there was always the wise man, the shaman, *Väinämöinen*, to intercede on their behalf.

It was impossible to separate nature from its religious context. The old beliefs were so much a part of everyday life that Christianity found it difficult to counter them. Christianity spread to Finland from both east and west towards the end of the first millennium AD. The ancient rituals associated with nature were transposed into celebrations of Christian feasts and saints.

Although the Reformation in the 1520s officially swept the old Catholic saints away, the ancient legends and traditions survived

**In the old days a variety of decorative wooden implements were given the bride by the groom. The picture shows a mangle board, distaff head and a woven *käspaikka* or hand towel, which was also used in religious ceremonies.**

and even thrived among the common people. For example, on December 26th, *Tapanin-päivä*, it was the custom to ride in sledges drawn by foals

harnessed for the first time. This was, after all, St. Stephen's day, the patron saint of horses. July 27th, Sleepyhead Day, *Unikeonpäivä*, commemorated the legend of the seven martyrs of Ephesus who fled from the emperor Decius and spent the years from 249–447 asleep in a cave. According to the custom, anyone who slept late on this day would be tired for the rest of the year. This day is still celebrated in Hanko and Naantali.

*Laskiainen*, Shrove Tuesday, is celebrated seven weeks before Easter, but many of the customs associated with it are very ancient and concern work, signifying the last day of the annual work cycle. Easter, despite its Christian origin, contains elements linking it to ancient Finnish customs, such as preventing witches and evil spirits harming the cattle by lighting bonfires. Certain areas still have their Easter bonfires, but mostly the tradition has changed. Nowadays, young girls, dressed as witches and armed with willow twigs decorated with coloured paper and feathers, go from house to house wishing people good luck and prosperity.

Bonfires at Midsummer, St. John the Baptist's Day, *Juhannus*, are strangely thought to be early Christian in origin, but many old folk traditions are associated with this magical nightless day. It is the celebration of growth,

**Of all the traditional Midsummer bonfires, the biggest in the Helsinki area is at the Seurasaari openair museum.**

Irma Kukkasjärvi's "Taiwa" ryijy rug.

fertility. In most areas doorways are still decorated with young birch trees and magnificent Midsummer poles are raised in the Åland Islands. Cattle were bedecked with garlands of flowers and young maidens placed a sprig of nine herbs under their pillows so they would dream of their future bridegrooms. Naked girls rolled in the dewy grass because they believed it to be a powerful ahprodisiac, and when they looked into a pool they would see the face of their beloved. Many of these old customs have been kept alive because they provide people with fun and amusement.

Christmas, *joulu*, was, and still is, the most important feast of the year. Originally, it signified the completion of the harvest year, and thus is celebrated with such traditional foods as salmon, roast pork, stockfish, sausages, vegetable casseroles, rice pudding, prune pies, and home-brewed beer. The idea of the Christmas tree spread rapidly in the last century, and is perhaps the most important element of the Finnish Christmas.

Originally, the Finnish Father Christmas, *joulupukki*, took the form of a goat, or of a man disguised as a goat, who went from house to house throwing presents in through the doorways. However, following a children's radio programme in 1927, the present day Father Christmas, with his Korvatunturi home in Finnish Lapland, took shape to the lasting delight of children throughout the world.

Folklore traditions and customs survived into the early part of this century, and even folk art retained its original forms. It took time before industrialisation penetrated the distant rural areas, so peasant culture survived intact. The life of the peasant was tied to the seasons, and his close observation of nature gave rise to an ability to forecast the weather. From this came the old sayings and beliefs that have been handed down from one generation to the next. There are still those who forecast the weather according to ancient traditions and natural signs.

### TRADITIONAL HANDICRAFTS

Customs related to weddings have been important in upholding old traditions in handicrafts and folk art. Young girls made the textiles, linen and dresses for their own trousseaus, stored in a beautifully decorated and painted trunk. These she would show to a prospective suitor as proof of her skills and abilities.

The bridegroom, too, made presents for his bride. The most popular, especially in the western areas, were beautifully and intricately carved wooden objects like distaffs, mangle rollers, and different kinds of boxes and trunks. Old handicraft traditions have proved most resilient and have recently undergone a revival.

Finnish handicrafts first won international recognition when a *ryijy* rug was sent to the Swedish court in the 16th century. This was of the natural dyed, napped-type known in Scandinavia since the Bronze Age, and used as a cover with the nap side downwards. In 1900, the Flame *ryijy* designed by Akseli Gallen-Kallela won a gold medal at the Paris World Fair, and since the 1950s modern Finnish *ryijy* rugs have received increasing international recognition.

Handicraft traditions also include the making of a wide range of national costumes. The varieties and colours can be traced back to prehistoric times. It is now quite fashionable to wear a selfmade national costume to parties.

### SAMI CULTURE

The Samis are the people living in the far north of Fennoscandia, and the oldest known inhabitants of that area. Their language, *Sami*, belongs to the Fenno-Ugrian family, and Sami culture is based on a pastoral way of life. To preserve and advance Sami culture and language, the Nordic countries set up the Nordic Sami Institute in 1973.

For the Samis the reindeer is a multi-purpose beast: it draws their sledges, carries their goods, provides meat and milk, and skins for clothes and tents.

The Sami people are expert hunters and fishers. Their traditional dwelling is the transportable *kota*, a pole frame covered with skins, and insulated in winter with woven wool rugs. The numerous Sami national costumes, rarely seen these days, are extremely colourful affairs. Furs are extensively used in winter for coats, leggings and mittens.

The culture of the Orthodox Skolt Lapps, who moved from the Kola Peninsula and Petsamo areas during the last war, is quite different from that of the other Sami people.

### LITERATURE

The oldest Finnish literature consists of the epic poems, folk legends and stories, and proverbs handed down by oral tradition. The written language was created by Mikael Agricola (1510–1557), who translated the New Testament, part of the Old Testament, and wrote the first Finnish ABC. Until the early 19th century, most works in Finnish were of a religious or popular educational nature, fiction being written in Swedish. Afterwards a deliberate movement to promote a Finnish culture and literature got underway. This was led by the statesman and philosopher J.V. Snellman (1806–1881) and the folklorist Elias Lönnrot (1802–1884). The Finnish Literature Society (established 1831) awarded Lönnrot a travel scholarship to enable him to continue collecting folklore. In 1835 the Society published his collection of epic folk poetry *Kalevala*, which was to become the very foundation of Finnish culture. In creating this great saga out of the oral runes he had collected, Lönnrot provided the nation with both a history and a literature. The *Kalevala* has been translated into almost 40 languages and is beyond doubt the best-known work of Finnish literature abroad.

With his *Tales of the Ensign Ståhl*, J.L. Runeberg (1804–1877) considerably influenced the rise of Finnish self-esteem and national identity; the poem "Our Land" in the book providing the words for the national anthem.

Although best known for his fairy tales, Zacharias Topelius (1818–1898) played an important role in awakening a sense of patriotism and history, and writing textbooks that were long used in the schools.

The period of Late Romanticism (1860–1880) produced Finland's most important author, Aleksis Kivi (1834–1872), the founder of modern Finnish literature. His epic romance *Seitsemän veljestä*, Seven Brothers, (1870) (translated into over 20 languages) and his plays are unsurpassed masters of prose and drama. His *Nummisuutarit*, The Village Cobblers, remains the finest comedy in the Finnish language.

The Realism of the 1880s embraces Minna Canth's (1844–1897) stark exposures of the injustices suffered by the working class and women, Juhani Aho's (1861–1921) portrayals of nature and ordinary folk, and Teuvo Pakkala's (1862–1925) descriptions of the life of the poor and children in small towns.

Karelianism, the dominant force at the turn of the century, drew its inspiration from the untouched wildernesses and rune lands of Karelia. The period exerted a considerable influence on the poet Eino Leino (1878–1926), clearly recognisable in the lines of his *Whitsongs*. The leading narrative writers of the first decade of the present century were Johannes Linnankoski (1869–1913), Ilmari Kianto (1874–1970), Joel Lehtonen (1881–1931) and F.E. Sillanpää (1888–1964). Sillanpää, whose works are imbued with a sympathetic and optimistic view of the world, received the Nobel Prize for literature in 1939. His major works are *Meek Heritage* (1919) and *The Maid Silja* (1931). Maria Jotuni (1880–1943) was one of the leading writers of plays and short stories at that time. Swedish-language literature, especially poetry, experienced a major breakthrough in the lyrics of Edith Södergran (1892–1923), the pioneer of modernism in Finland.

Mikael Agricola (1510–1557)

Elias Lönnrot (1802–1884)

J.L. Runeberg (1804–1877)

Aleksis Kivi (1834–1872)

**Edith Södergran (1882– 1923)**  **Eino Leino (1878–1926)**  **F.E. Sillanpää (1888– 1964)**

**Mika Waltari (1908–1979)**  **Väinö Linna (1920–1992)**  **Eeva-Liisa Manner (1921–)**

**Pentti Saarikoski (1937– 1983)**  **Paavo Haavikko (1931–)**  **Eeva Joenpelto (1921–)**

In more recent times, Mika Waltari (1908–1979) achieved international success. His great historical novels (like *The Egyptian*, which has also been filmed) have been translated into over 20 languages. Other significant novelists were Pentti Haanpää (1906–1955) with his portrayals of country people, nature and animals, and Toivo Pekkanen (1902–1957) for his descriptions of life in industrial society.

The Winter and Continuation Wars, territorial concessions, and the transformation of the country's internal and foreign situation, caused much self-searching and re-evaluation among writers. The leading representative of this new trend is Väinö Linna (1920–1992), whose novel *The Unknown Soldier* (1954) dealt with war in a refreshingly new and honest way through the eyes of an ordinary soldier. The book, which has sold over 600 000 copies and been adapted twice for the cinema, has been an unprecedented success. Linna's triology *Täällä Pohjantähden alla* (Here under the Northern Star) (1959–1962) is a socio-historical novel of a Finnish community over the past hundred years.

Veijo Meri (1928–) is one of the modernising forces in Finnish prose, and *The Manila Rope* (1957) is perhaps his best-known novel abroad. A close contemporary, Paavo Rintala (1930–), has combined a traditional with a more modern approach in his description of war. Eeva Joenpelto's (1921–) most important work is her Lohja series, a portrayal of the lives of a group of people between the wars.

The leading figures in post-war literature in Swedish are Tito Colliander (1904–1989), Christer Kihlman (1930–), Henrik Tikkanen (1924–1984), the 1986 Finlandia Prize winner Jörn Donner (1933–), and Göran Schildt (1917–), the travel writer and biographer of Alvar Aalto. The Moomin family books of Tove Jansson (1914–), translated into almost 30 languages, have delighted children in all corners of the world.

Mainstream prose in the 1960s and 1970s was concerned with life among workers, the middle-class and the modernising countryside. The naturalistic, left-wing writer Hannu Salama (1936–) has produced the most vivid portrayals of the working-class milieu. Others writing in the same vein are Alpo Ruuth (1943–) and Lasse Sinkkonen (1937–1976).

Swedish-language prose has long concerned itself with the crisis of middle-class life, as the works of Kihlman and Tikkanen show. The same theme has been dealt with in Finnish by Kerttu-Kaarina Suosalmi (1921–), Anu Kaipainen (1933–) and Eeva Kilpi (1928–). In his novels and short stories, Antti Tuuri (1944–) uses

**"And what do you think happened then?"** Tove Jansson's beloved Moomin and Little My picking berries in summertime with Moomin Mother.

industrialists and engineers to convey his view of the world and social change. Other novels, several of which have been filmed, have been about war and emigration.

With increasing internationalisation and urbanisation, readers have turned to descriptions of country life, to the works of Kalle Päätalo (1919–). In his series of autobiographical novels he paints a detailed picture of the

transformation of rural life. Eino Säisä (1935–1988) dealt with the same theme in his own series of novels. So different and unique were the writings of Timo K. Mukka (1944–1973) that it is difficult to categorise them. The setting for his greatest novel, *Maa on syntinen laulu* (The Earth is a Sinful Song), is the North, the theme is love, religion and death. This was made into a highly successful film that even won international recognition. The satirist Erno Paasilinna (1935–) won the first Finlandia Prize in 1985 for a collection of essays. The poet Nils-Aslak Valkeapää (1943–) has pioneered the culture of his own people, the Samis.

The radical transformation of poetry in the 1950s was spearheaded by the works of Aila Meriluoto (1924–) and Lauri Viita (1916–1965). Other representatives of the new poetry include Helvi Juvonen (1919–1959), the critic Tuomas Anhava (1927–), Eeva-Liisa Manner (1921–), Eila Kivikk'aho (1921–) and the author, member of the Academy of Finland and publisher Paavo Haavikko (1931–).

Paavo Haavikko is probably the most original poet of his generation. His widely translated *Selected Poems* includes such brilliance that one can justifiably call him a genius. Haavikko is also a master of the novel, play, aphorism and historical essay. In 1984 he was awarded the much coveted Neustadt Prize for Literature.

Pentti Saarikoski (1937–1983) was often called the *enfant terrible* of Finnish literature. With his *Mitä tapahtuu todella?* (What happens really?) in 1962 he began a new chapter in political poetry. Saarikoski was also a gifted translator, skillfully rendering into Finnish the Greek and Latin classics, as well as modern writers like Joyce and Sallinger. His extensive knowledge was also reflected in his poetry, considered to be among the best ever written in Finland. The works of Saarikoski and other poets have been translated into English by Anselm Hollo

(1934–), a poet himself who mainly writes in English. Other notable modern poets are Sirkka Turkka (1939–) and Arto Melleri (1956–).

It is worth while mentioning that each year Finnish publishers bring out a considerable number of firsts by hitherto unknown poets, which is one indication of the high regard poetry has in Finnish literature.

Among the best post-war Finnish-Swedish poets are Solveig von Schoultz (1907–), the author Bo Carpelan (1926–), Lars Huldén (1926–), the modernist Claes Andersson (1937–), Finlandia-prize winner Gösta

**Tampere City Library, designed by Raili and Reima Pietilä, and completed in 1986. It has the shape of the capercaillie it is named after.**

Ågren (1936–) and the versatile Märta Tikkanen (1935–), who has received international recognition for her woman's interpretation of the world.

Writers in Finland are supported by the state through a system of grants, some of them for a number of years. Of the many prizes for literature, the Finlandia, awarded separately for fiction and non-fiction, is the biggest: both are worth FIM 100 000.

According to the latest UNESCO statistics Finland published more titles per 10 000 inhabitants than any other country in the world. The figure was 17.1, whereas that for the United States was only 1.2 per 10 000. Translated books account for about a half of the total, and most of them are from English.

### LIBRARIES

As Finns are among the most avid readers in the world, it is fortunate that they have a widespread network of libraries. The network includes over 1500 municipal-owned public libraries, with a fleet of bookmobiles servicing over 18 000 stopping points. Thus it is possible to borrow books and recordings from more than 20 000 places. The state also supports these libraries, in addition to some 600 scientific libraries and information centres.

At present the public libraries have more than 30 million books, a million recordings, and a growing video service. The scientific libraries have over 15 million volumes. These services are open to almost everyone, including resident foreigners.

The average borrowing rate from the public libraries is 18 books or recordings a year, making a total by 1989 of 81 million. The figure for scientific library borrowings is 3 million. Libraries also arrange literary evenings and children's events, operate an inter-lending service, and are developing an information retrieval service network.

Finland has for long been a pioneer in library building, and the two new central libraries completed in Helsinki and Tampere in 1986 have continued this tradition. Designed by Kaarlo Leppänen and Raili and Reima Pietilä respectively, they are both architecturally and functionally exceptional.

## MUSIC

Finnish folk music has a long and rich tradition, which is kept alive through such annual festivals as that at Kaustinen. Finnish composers, too, have drawn their inspiration from folk music. The country's musical life, though diverse and vigorous, is, however, comparatively new. Nevertheless, performers and composers have given it a worthy reputation abroad.

Not until the end of the 18th century were there Finnish composers known by name. In the following century the leading figure was Fredrik Pacius. He organised the first orchestra and choir in Helsinki, wrote a number of operas, and set the national anthem "Our Land" to music. Jean Sibelius (1865–1957), already a foremost composer by the end of the 19th century, became a major symphonist in the early decades of this century. His extensive output includes seven symphonies, symphonic poems and orchestral suites inspired by ancient Finnish themes, an opera and a number of elegant minor works. Erik Tawaststjerna was the leading authority in the world on Sibelius, and his biography of the master has been translated into English.

Although many of the Finnish composers of this period worked in the shadow of Sibelius, they still managed to make a significant contribution to the country's music. Among them are Erkki Melartin, a productive writer of minature compositions, Toivo Kuula, whose tragic early death

The young Jean Sibelius, Eero Järnefelt's portrait from 1894.

Aino Ackté was an international opera singer of repute at the beginning of the century. Albert Edelfelt's painting from 1901.

cut short a career as a composer of songs for choir and solo voice, Selim Palmgren, the composer of piano and male choir music, the symphonist and opera composer Leevi Madetoja and the modernist Aarre Merikanto.

The symphonic poems of Uuno Klami resound with nationalist and impressionistic overtones. Yrjö Kilpinen is one of the greatest lied composers of the century.

In more recent times Erik Bergman has breathed new life into Finnish choral music and received international recognition for his vocal works. Einar Englund is well-known for his symphonies and piano concertos, and the versatile Einojuhani Rautavaara has won many international prizes with his compositions. Bengt Johansson, Finland's first composer of electronic music, inspired others to follow in this field. Among the leading lights of the younger generation are the symphonist and opera composer Paavo Heininen, the composer and scholar Erkki Salmenhaara, the symphonist and concerto composer Pehr Henrik Nordgren, composer and conductor Esa-Pekka Salonen and the gifted symphonist Kalevi Aho. Composers of computer music include Kaija Saariaho, Jukka Tiensuu and Magnus Lindberg.

Finnish opera underwent a

**The soprano Karita Mattila has sung in many famous opera houses in the world. This picture was taken after a performance of *Don Giovanni* at the New York Metropolitan.**

The Savonlinna Opera
Festival is one of the main
cultural events of the summer.
The picture is from Aulis Sallinen's
opera *The King Goes Forth to France*.

renaissance in the seventies and eighties with the appearance of Joonas Kokkonen's *The Last Temptations*, Aulis Sallinen's *The Red Line* and *The Horseman*, and Paavo Heininen's *The Silk Drum* and *The Knife*. Opera has reached an ever widening section of the public through internationally important festivals at Savonlinna and Ilmajoki. Finnish opera has enjoyed an unprecedented success on the leading opera stages of the world like London and New York. World fame has come to many individual opera singers, starting at the beginning of the century with Aino Ackté, the soprano and founder of the Savonlinna Opera Festival, to the basses Martti Talvela, Jaakko Ryhänen and Matti Salminen, the baritone Jorma Hynninen and the sopranos Anita Välkki, Taru Valjakka and Karita Mattila.

Instrumentalists of national, and even international importance, include the pianists Ralf Gothóni, Eero Heinonen and Erik T. Tawaststjerna, and the cellist Arto Noras. The leading conductors include Paavo Berglund, Ulf Söderblom, Jorma Panula, Leif Segerstam, Okko Kamu, Esa-Pekka Salonen and Jukka-Pekka Saraste.

Jazz came to Finland fairly late, but thanks to the increase in foreign contacts, its position has gradually strengthened. Among the many musicians known abroad are saxophonist Eero Koivistoinen, guitarists Jukka Tolonen and Pekka Pohjala, trumpeter Simo Salminen, drummer Jukka-Pekka Uotila, composers and pianists Heikki Sarmanto and Jukka Linkola, and double-bass player Teppo Hauta-aho.

The main jazz event of the year, the Pori Jazz Festival, is important enough to attract top international performers like Lionel Hampton, Oscar Peterson and Miles Davis.

Light music, whether played live by dance bands or on the radio and TV, continues to retain its great popularity. The most productive light music composer was Toivo Kärki, whose career extended over many decades. In the golden twenties comic songs were all the vogue; Alfred Tanner was the leading performer and Dallapé the best known dance band. Since then there have been many popular singers like Georg Malmstén, Tapio Rautavaara, Olavi Virta, Mauno Kuusisto, Marion Rung, M.A. Numminen, Hector, Tapani Kansa, Danny, Katri-Helena, Anneli Saaristo and Arja Saionmaa. The top rock musicians have been Tuomari Nurmio and Juice Leskinen, and the top groups Broadcast, Hurriganes, Sielun Veljet, Eppu Normaali and Lapinlahden Linnut, few of whom even earned a reputation abroad. One such was Hanoi Rocks, which broke up a few years back, and another the Havana Blacks.

## DANCE

In 1922 Edvard Fazer set up the Finnish National Ballet as part of the Finnish National Opera founded eleven years earlier. For the company's premiere, ballet masters George Gé and Alexander Saxelin produced *Swan Lake* in the spirit of Russian classical ballet.

The Finnish National Opera has its own ballet school, with an almost completely Finnish staff and a corps de ballet of

**Finnish National Ballet dancers Kirsi and Jukka Aromaa have won many prizes in international ballet competitions.**

almost 60 dancers. The Helsinki City Theatre also has its own dance group, and there are several other smaller ones in the provinces.

The director of the Finnish National Ballet from 1984 to 1991 was Doris Laine and since 1991 Jorma Uotinen, both versatile

Maija Lavonen's "Path"
ryijy rug.

Tapio Wirkkala's "Trunk"
vase.

and gifted dancers and familiar visitors on many foreign stages.

The other leading light of Finnish dance is Margaretha von Bahr, still working as a teacher and choreographer. She runs a private ballet school in Helsinki, and many of her students have won important prizes abroad.

Jorma Uotinen is considered to have revolutionised Finnish dance. He began with the National Ballet, transferred to modern ballet and was for many years a member of Carolyn Carlson's GRCOP dance group. Today he is the best-known Finnish choreographer abroad. He has successfully danced and presented his own works in many European countries.

The new generation of promising young dancers includes Jukka and Kirsi Aromaa, the brother and sister team who have won many international prizes.

The international reputation of Finnish dance has been much helped by the annual Kuopio Dance and Music Festival, the only one of its kind in Scandinavia. This is one of the most exciting of the summer events organised by Finland Festivals.

**DESIGN**

The unique element in Finnish design is its closeness to nature. Nature has provided the motifs, shapes, colours, materials, and even influenced the treatment of materials.

Water is an essential part of Finnish nature, and the curving shores of lakes have inspired many works of art, like Alvar Aalto's famous Savoy vase. The play of light and colour in the changing seasons is reflected in the textiles, ryijy and raanu rugs of Irma Kukkasjärvi, Uhra Simberg-Ehrström, Elsa Montell-Saanio and Maija Lavonen, some ablaze with colours, others subtle and calm. Glass designers retain a predilection for flora and fauna motifs. Wood, however, remains the most popular material. The deep affection Finns have for the forests helps designers working by hand to express and accentuate its natural characteristics.

In the works of ceramic artists like Birger Kaipainen and Rut Bryk there is a clear Byzantine presence, although later on Bryk has become distinctly modernist.

When the teaching of design first began in the last century, one of the inspirations was national identity. Finnish design made its international debut at the Paris World Exhibition in 1900. In 1951 the American journal *House Beautiful* thought Tapio Wirkkala's wooden vase the most beautiful object in the world, and a few years later Timo Sarpaneva's glass sculpture was awarded the same honour.

Quality design is timeless. The furniture designed by Alvar Aalto between the wars, and the works

**Steel fondue set and plastic containers designed by Timo Sarpaneva.**

of many other designers from the fifties are still in production, selling well, and still as modern looking.

The fifties was the era of the star designers producing their one-off's or small runs. Nowadays, the emphasis is more on utility articles within the reach of all. The highly original yet practical design concept behind Marimekko's frocks and textiles ensured instant success at home and abroad. Vuokko Nurmesniemi, who started with Marimekko, went on to found her own company, producing similar, even more elegant dresses and textiles. Kaj Frank began in the fifties designing faience tableware, then moved on to other materials, even plastics. Heikki Orvola has created some fine and functional enamel kitchenware, as well as sculpturing in glass, and Oiva Toikka both utility and art objects in glass. Tapio Wirkkala was one of the greatest and most versatile designers this country has ever produced, equally at home with glass, metal, wood and porcelain. Timo Sarpeneva produces some artistic yet practical glass objects, nowadays very highly valued, and also utility articles in porcelain, cast iron, steel and plastic, and has even designed clothes. The silversmith Bertel Gardberg revolutionised metalworking in Finland, producing beautiful and simple cutlery in silver and steel, and some exquisite silver objects. Antti Nurmesniemi and Yrjö Kukkapuro are the top names in interior design. Both they and Simo Heikkilä have a fine reputation as furniture designers. Pirkko Stenros is known for her safe and practical furniture for children and Stefan Lindfors has made a name for himself as a furniture and lamp designer.

In the world of fashion, the top designers today are Markku Piri in textiles, Isa Kukkapuro in clothes, Pertti Palmroth in footwear, Björn Weckström in jewellery, and Tua Rahikainen in furs.

The considerable achievements of Finnish industry would not be possible today without the know-how and artistic talents of the professional designers they employ.

## THEATRE

The great popularity of the dramatic arts in Finland has its origins in old folk customs. Ancient rites to do with fishing and hunting, especially of bears, were carried over into wedding celebrations. Christianity, however, destroyed these old pagan customs, the church using dramatics for its own purposes and even taking it into the schools. The first theatrical performances in Finnish were in Turku in the 1650s, and the first theatres were built in the 19th century. Pietari Hannikainen's

*Silmänkääntäjät* (The Conjurers), first performed in 1847, was the first play written in Finnish. The true beginning of Finnish-language theatre is, however, Aleksis Kivi's *Lea*, which had its first night in Helsinki in 1869. The National Theatre was founded in 1872. In addition to the professional theatre, Finland also has an extremely active amateur theatrical movement.

There are over 40 professional theatres in the country, and a considerable number of semi-professional and amateur theatres, summer theatres, student and youth groups. In terms of the number of theatres and the size of audiences, Finland is one of the leading countries in Europe. Frequent exchange visits are made between Finnish and foreign theatres. Of the many gifted

**Wäinö Aaltonen's statue of the writer Aleksis Kivi occupies a place of honour outside the Finnish National Theatre.**

directors, Vivica Bandler, Lasse Pöysti, Ralf Långbacka, Jack Witikka and Kalle Holmberg are perhaps the best known in Scandinavia. Undoubtedly the most gifted and controversial figure in modern Finnish theatre is Jouko Turkka, who is both a director and teacher. The leading school is the Academy of Dramatic Art in Helsinki, which also has a Swedish-language department.

Radio plays continue to fulfil an important role, as do the television theatres of the state and commercial networks.

Both Finnish and foreign plays are included in the extensive repertoires. Greater interest has been shown recently in politically and socially committed theatre. An overview of the dramatic arts is provided each year by the well-attended Tampere Theatre Festival, organised by Finland Festivals.

Since Finland became a member of the International Theatre Institute in 1950 its international ties have grown enormously.

### CINEMA

Regular film production began in Finland in 1906, and the first talkie was made in 1931. Output fell off sharply with the arrival of television, but also because of over production and changed leisure habits. In the 1980s an average of 15 feature films were made each year, as well as a considerable number of TV movies, shorts, documentaries and animated films. Film production is supported by the Finnish Film Foundation funded jointly by the Ministry of Education and the film industry.

Among the few internationally-known film directors are Jörn Donner, whose versatile production includes a documentary on Ingmar Bergman, and Rauni Mollberg, whose *Maa on syntinen laulu* (The Earth is a Sinful Song)

Film director Rauni Mollberg (centre) made a new version of Väinö Linna's *The Unknown Soldier* in 1985. The film depicts the Continuation War through the eyes of young soldiers. Although the new film was well received, it was not so unanimously acclaimed as Edvin Laine's original version.

Helsinki railway station, built between 1904 and 1919, is perhaps Eliel Saarinen's most famous building. On both sides of the main entrance are Emil Wikström's impressive "Torch Bearers".

has been successfully shown abroad. The Kaurismäki brothers, Aki and Mika, have almost become cult figures in Europe and the USA, their latest films even being made abroad. The most popular Finnish film of all time is Edvin Laine's adaptation of Väinö Linna's novel *Tuntematon sotilas* (The Unknown Solider), a new version of which was made by Mollberg in 1985. The *Uuno Turhapuro* (Uuno Uselessbrook) films by Ere Kokkonen have been continuously popular among Finns, mainly because Uuno is considered to represent the sterotype Finnish male. Other important directors are Pertti "Spede" Pasanen, the late Mikko Niskanen, Pirjo Honkasalo and the Pekka Lehto Group, Anssi Mänttäri, Pekka Parikka, Heikki Partanen and Markku Lehmuskallio. Renny Harlin, who was never a success in Finland, made a good career for himself as a Hollywood producer and director.

## ARCHITECTURE

Finland's oldest architectural monuments are its medieval stone castles and churches, and intricately carved, folk-built wooden churches and bell-towers from the 18th century. The greatest name in the early 19th century was C.L. Engel (1778–1840), who created the magnificent, uniform Neo-Classical centre of Helsinki.

National Romanticism, the

dominant style at the turn of the century, contained influences from Karelian wooden architecture, medieval stone building, and the rich ornamentation of European Jugend Stil or Art Nouveau. The leading architects of the period were Eliel Saarinen (1873–1950), Herman Gesellius (1874–1916), Armas Lindgren (1874–1929) and Lars Sonck (1870–1956). They designed both private houses and important public buildings, like the Helsinki Railway Station by Eliel Saarinen. This was probably his greatest work before leaving for the United States in 1923 to enrichen its architecture. The twenties were dominated by the more severe lines of classicism and a struggle for a more rational style, the most monumental expression of which is J.S. Sirén's (1889–1961) Parliament building.

The breakthrough of functionalism came at the end of the 1920s with the works of Erik Bryggman (1891–1955) and Alvar Aalto (1898–1976), the greatest name in modern Finnish architecture. Internationally, Aalto is recognised as one of the great modernisers of architecture, whose influence is felt in urban and regional planning, interior and industrial design.

After the post-functionalism of Viljo Revell, Heikki Siren and Aulis Blomstedt, Alvar Aalto's individualistic white period and Reima Pietilä's unique expressionism, the seventies turned to constructivism, which stressed the social role of architecture. The urgent need for housing was met through serial production and prefabrication. In practice this often meant that a good idea became abominable architecture; only a few schemes, such as the Olari suburb by Simo Järvinen and Eero Valjakka, could be con-sidered successful.

The 1980s saw the return to good architecture, in which the emphasis has been on humanism and environmental harmony, recalling the very best ideas of the now classic Tapiola Garden City from the 1950s. The timelessness of architecture has been accentuated in the restoration of old buildings and historic milieus, of which Katajanokka in Helsinki is perhaps one of the finest examples. Oulunsalo Town Hall, designed by the NVV office, is a good example of the new regionalism in architecture. Lahti City Theatre, completed in 1983 from a design by Pekka Salminen, is a monument to modernism, a successful blend of concrete and humanism.

**Ilmo Valjakka's post-modernist design for Yhtyneet Kuvalehdet publishing house (completed in 1987) has a glass-roofed atrium. Landscape offices have been replaced by glass-doored rooms.**

Reima and Raili Pietilä's, projects include the Finnish Embassy in New Delhi, Tampere City Library, and the president's official residence.

Finnish architects continue to do well in invited competitions abroad, and have made a major contribution to export projects as these often require everything from design to construction.

**PAINTING**

The oldest examples of art in Finland are the numerous Stone Age rock engravings of Arctic hunting culture, and medieval frescoes in the stone churches of Åland, Lohja and Hattula, and the wooden churches of Ostrobothnia.

It was only with the establishment of the Fine Arts Society of Finland in 1848 that Finnish art really came into existence. Folk poetry and the *Kalevala* provided the inspiration for the national themes of R.W. Ekman (1808–1873). The three von Wright brothers, Magnus (1805–1868), Wilhelm (1810–1887) and Ferdinand (1822–1906), painting largely in the Biedermeier spirit, are best known for their meticulous studies of fauna, but even their landscapes are considered masterpieces. The Düsseldorf School is represented by the landscape artist Werner Holmberg (1830–1860).

The true flourishing of Finnish art came towards the end of the 19th century, a golden age in which the influences of French naturalism were mixed with homespun national-romanticism, synthetism and early Italian Renaissance forms. The leading names of the period are the history painter Albert Edelfelt (1854–1905), and Finland's most versatile artist Akseli Gallen-Kallela (1865–1931), who found his inspiration as much in the *Kalevala* as in the nature and people of the untouched wilderness. Eero Järnefelt (1863–1937) is known for his sophisticated depictions of the common people and fine portraits. Pekka Halonen (1865–1933) painted both monumental studies of the people and elegant, decorative landscapes. Juha Rissanen (1873–1950) painted ordinary people with a forceful monumentalism and subtle humour.

The main representatives of symbolism were Magnus Enckell (1870–1925) and Hugo Simberg (1873–1917). In the early years of this century two groups were established. The Septem Group in 1912, which was led by Magnus Enckell and inspired by French Post-Impressionism. The central figure of the expressionist November Group formed in 1917 was Tyko Sallinen (1879–1955),

**Designs by Reima and Raili Pietilä often reflect the contours of the Finnish landscape, as in Mäntyniemi, the presidential residence.**

**Albert Edelfelt's scene from the Club War, "The Burned Village", powerfully portrays the depth of human fear.**

considered the founder of modern, national art. Though painting in a totally different way from Sallinen, Helene Schjerfbeck (1862–1946) can also be considered an expressionist. Her later works in particular possess a highly individual restraint and inner power. The first naïvists were Sulho Sipilä (1895–1949) and Vilho Lampi (1898–1936). Otto Mäkilä (1904–1955) became the central figure in the surrealist movement when it appeared in the twenties, but later, like other surrealists, he became an abstractionist. The spiritual heir to the November Group was the October Group, set up in 1933.

It was inspired by Aimo Kanerva (1909–1991), who was best known for his powerfully expressive oil and watercolour landscapes and portraits. The October Group also includes Unto Koistinen (1917–1994), whose portraits and female studies possess an imaginative and expressive quality.

In recent decades Finnish art has followed the international "isms" without losing its specifically national character. The dark-toned Ostrobothnian landscapes and interiors of Veikko Vionoja (1909–) and

**Strong, joyful colours speak out in "Street Scene", Rafael Wardi's oil painting from 1988.**

**Many of Hannu Väisänen's themes are taken from literature, as here in "Orpheus Playing".**

**The sculptress Eila Hiltunen's main work, the 24-ton Sibelius monument.**

the dominant greens in Olli Miettinen's (1899–1969) rural scenes possess a characteristically fresh Nordic touch. An early representative of concretism was Birger Carlstedt (1907–1975), but its greatest exponent was Sam Vanni (1908–1992), the central figure in the Prisma Group set up in the 1950s. Among the many abstract painters, special mention can be made of Per Stenius (1922–)

and Anitra Lucander (1918–). The foremost surrealists of today are Alpo Jaakola (1929–) and Juhani Linnovaara (1934–); the Lapp artist Reidar Särestöniemi (1925–1981) can also be considered a surrealist. The main representatives of neo-realism in the 1960s and 1970s are Jaakko Sievänen (1932–), Esko Tirronen (1934–), Juhani Harri (1939–), and Kimmo Kaivanto (1932–), who is also known for his graphics and sculptures.

The most famous illustrator of children's books in Finland was Rudolf Koivu (1890–1946). Erkki

Tanttu (1907–1985) became a legend with his illustrations of folk humour, Björn Landström (1917–) for his drawings of ships, and Kari Suomalainen (1920–) for his satirical political cartoons.

The graphic arts flourished again in the 1950s in the wake of the international recognition accorded to Finnish design. A whole new generation came into being, with people like Ernst Mether-Borgström and Tuulikki Pietilä providing a new and vital artistic expression. The leading graphic artists today, Pentti Kaskipuro (1930–) and Pentti Lumikangas (1926–), are recognised for their highly personal styles.

### SCULPTURE

Very few of the works of early Finnish sculptors have survived. The most valuable wooden sculptures in medieval Finnish churches actually come from Gotland, Germany and the Netherlands. The oldest known Finnish medieval sculptor was the Master of Lieto.

The early pioneers were Erik Cainberg (1771–1816), who first used *Kalevala* motifs, and Carl

Eneas Sjöstrand (1828–1906), whose realistic works had an enduring influence on embryonic Finnish sculpture. The main works of the classicist Walter Runeberg (1838–1920) are the statue to J.L. Runeberg (1885) in Esplanade park, Helsinki, and to Alexander II (1894) in Senate Square, Helsinki. Johannes Takanen's (1848–1885) talented works, especially his female and child figures, possess a natural plasticity and charm. Robert Stigell (1852–1907) leaned towards realism and the baroque, and his best known work is The Shipwrecked (1898) on the Observatory Hill in Helsinki. Perhaps the most gifted and individual sculptor was Ville Vallgren (1855–1940), whose output includes both massive public works and graceful miniature figures from fired clay in the Art Nouveau spirit. His most beloved work is the Havis Amanda fountain (1908) in Helsinki's market square, whose audacious Frenchiness aroused such a storm when first unveiled.

Undoubtedly the leading name in modern Finnish sculpture was Wäinö Aaltonen (1894–1966). He worked in bronze, ceramics and marble, but more importantly in granite – the first to use this element since the ancient Egyptians. Depending on the material used one of two features characterise his works: either a powerful monumentalism or a masculine lyricism. His main works are the statue to Aleksis Kivi (1939) in the Railway Square, Helsinki, the four figures (1929) on Hämeensilta Bridge, Tampere, the statue to Paavo Nurmi (1924) outside the Olympic Stadium, and the classical figures (1938) in the chamber of the Parliament building. Aimo Tukiainen (1917–) is a sculptor of memorials and busts, at first figurative but later abstract. Numerous cemeteries are adorned with his war memorials, but his most notable work is the equestrian statue of Marshal Mannerheim (1960) in Helsinki.

The modern scene is dominated by a number of highly expressive sculptresses. Eila Hiltunen (1922–) displays her original and imaginative versatility in welded metal fountains in Tampere and Helsinki, and the Sibelius Monument (1967) in Helsinki. The aesthetic Laila Pullinen (1933–) works in a combination of bronze and stone, and achieved a world reputation with her technique of exploding copper and bronze.

Kain Tapper (1930–), working mainly in wood, is one of the central figures of the expressionist, abstractionist trend. Others working in wood include Mauno Hartman (1930–) producing jointed logs inspired by the *Kalevala*, Eeva Ryynänen (1915–) with her massive human and animal forms, Heikki Viro-

The sculptor Tapio Junno was ''Artist of the Year'' in 1987. The picture is of his ''Moon Window''.

lainen (1936–) for his painted oak figures, and Alpo Jaakola (1929–) for his primitive wood sculptures and his paintings. An important young sculptress is Rauni Liukko (1940–), whose works are committed and subjective, repeatedly using such themes as women weighed down by labour, or children incarcerated in a violent and restrictive society.

Other socially critical young sculptors include Ossi Somma (1926–), Kimmo Kaivanto (1932–) and Kimmo Pyykkö (1940–).

# RADIO, TELEVISION AND THE PRESS

**RADIO AND THE HISTORY OF BROADCASTING**

Broadcasting began in Finland in 1923 when radio hams made their first transmissions. Suomen Yleisradio (Finnish Broadcasting Company), nowadays Oy Yleisradio Ab or YLE for short, was established in 1926 to produce and transmit radio programmes in Finnish and Swedish, the two official languages of the country.

The following year the Radio Act was passed, and this still regulates broadcasting in Finland. Broadcasting was placed under the Ministry of Communications and Public Works, the present Ministry of Transport and Communications. By the mid-fifties over half a

**In the early years of radio broadcasting the radio towers in Lahti were famous landmarks symbolising the growing importance of this new means of communication.**

**Finland has a dense network of magazine stalls, selling both Finnish and foreign publications.**

million licences had been issued, and today most households have one or more sets. YLE broadcasts 24 hours a day on three national stations and dozens of local ones.

Although YLE does not possess a *de jure* monopoly, in practice it has controlled broadcasting since the end of the last war. Since the mid-eighties, however, numerous local stations have come into existence, several of which are commercial.

### TELEVISION

It was also amateurs who pioneered television in Finland, this time the students of the

Tesvisio and Tamvisio, forming TV2 out of them.

In 1964 YLE became the only licensed broadcasting company in Finland for a period of twenty years. During this time MTV has had to broadcast on YLE channels. In 1985 YLE, MTV and Oy NOKIA Ab formed TV3 and began broadcasting on this new channel. In 1992 it was reserved solely for MTV broadcasts. Television programmes produced in Sweden have been transmitted in Finland on Channel 4 since 1988. Locally produced news and other Swedish-language programmes are transmitted on YLE channels. The countless number of English-language channels, Spanish, Italian, Estonian, Russian and the French TV5 relayed by satellite can be received by those with disks or linked to cable networks. The cable company PTV, which operates in the Greater Helsinki area, has more than 100 000 subscribers.

TV1, TV2 and TV3 are national networks, but TV4 can only be received in the coastal zone where most of the Swedish-speaking Finns live. Almost every household has at least one TV and that mainly in colour. VCRs have also become quite common.

The four channels broadcast some 200 hours a week. Almost half the programmes are locally produced, and these have high viewing ratings. The most

University of Technology in Helsinki, whose Tesvisio station was established in 1955. Within a year they and Tamvisio in Tampere had received operators' licences. To finance operations both companies sold advertising space. In spring 1957 another commercial company was set up, MTV, and together with YLE began regular transmissions that August. Later YLE bought out

popular of them are Finnish films and serials and entertainment programmes. Depending on the season, the average Finn watches between 9 and 14 hours a week, or 1 to 2 hours a day.

## THE PRESS

Finland's first newspaper appeared in Turku in 1771, and about the same time the first magazines saw the light of day. When Finland became a Grand Duchy in 1809 there was only one regularly published newspaper, and it was not until after the 1820s that more appeared. At first, these were in Swedish because their subscribers were Swedish-speaking. The oldest newspaper still being published is the Turku Swedish-language *Åbo Underrättelser*, founded in 1824. The oldest Finnish-language newspaper was *Uusi Suomi* dating from 1847.

According to UNESCO figures, the total circulation of Finnish dailies (that is newspapers appearing 3–7 times a week) in proportion to the population is the third highest in the world: 103 newspapers with a combined circulation of 3.28 million, or 660 copies per 1000 inhabitants. Approximately 6 % of these are in Swedish. In addition there are numerous locally published and freely distributed papers. Most Finns place an annual subscription for their newspaper, which is then delivered to their homes. Only the evening papers are bought from news stands.

There are ten newspapers which are considered national, although none of them have a truly nationwide coverage. The largest is *Helsingin Sanomat*, read by the majority of those living in the Helsinki area, but only by about 10 to 30 per cent elsewhere. There are two evening newspapers.

Although the share of the independents has grown, politically affiliated newspapers of the Left and Right continue to play an important role and account for almost half of total circulation. Most of the state subsidies paid to the press go to the party organs.

The exact number of magazines in Finland is impossible to estimate because, in addition to the regularly published ones, there is a long tradition of printing and distributing free opinion-forming publications. The Post Office reckons it delivers over 1100 magazines, the vast majority of them reviews, trade and professional journals.

## CIRCULATION OF NEWSPAPERS AND MAGAZINES

### Average circulation of leading newspapers, 1993

| | |
|---|---|
| Helsingin Sanomat (national, independent) | 486 856 |
| Ilta-Sanomat (evening) | 209 098 |
| Aamulehti (political) | 140 236 |
| Turun Sanomat(independent) | 127 850 |
| Maaseudun Tuelvaisuus (national) | 116 883 |
| Iltalehti (evening) | 116 036 |
| Kaleva (political) | 97 149 |
| Savon Sanomat(political) | 83 061 |
| Kauppalehti (financal) | 82 349 |
| Keskisuomalainen (political) | 82 080 |

### Average circulation of leading magazines, 1993

| | |
|---|---|
| Valitut Palat (Reader's Digest) | 345 866 |
| Aku Ankka (comic) | 299 432 |
| Seura (general interest) | 271 150 |
| Apu (general interest) | 252 912 |
| Kotiliesi (women) | 205 536 |
| Kotivinkki (women) | 201 391 |
| et-lehti (senior citizens) | 200 049 |
| Kodin Kuvalehti (women) | 178 773 |
| Anna (women) | 150 247 |
| Nykyposti (general interest) | 147 250 |

(Source: Levikintarkastus Oy).

# SPORT

## THE MOST POPULAR SPORTS

For centuries Finns have been keen on subjecting themselves to trials of strength, speed and agility. The Royal Academy of Turku had an instructor in swordmanship immediately it was established in 1640, sports became part of military life from the 1780s onwards, and the schools and universities showed a similar interest in the early 19th century. The first sports clubs came into existence in the 1850s.

Whether as participants or spectators, Finns take a serious interest in sport. In wintertime, pre-school kids and senior citizens alike go in for cross-country skiing. Slalom is increasing in popularity, especially among young people. Every weekend mass long-distance skiing events are organised, the greatest of which is the 75 km Finlandia Skiing Marathon from Hämeenlinna to Lahti in which over 10 000 enthusiasts participate. When summer comes the Finns start jogging, swimming, cycling, playing football and *pesäpallo*, the Finnish version of baseball. Orienteering is also very popular. As the country has a great number of swimming halls, people can swim throughout the winter. The games that draw the most spectators are ice hockey,

football, athletics and skiing. Trotting, car and motorbike racing, rally driving, ball games, golf and so on, are all quite popular and have no lack of participants or spectators.

## GREAT FINNISH VICTORIES

Finland first entered the Olympics at the intermediate games in Athens in 1906 where it also scored its first victory: Verner Weckman in wrestling. The country was still a Russian Grand Duchy when it took part in the Stockholm Olympics in 1912, this time winning 9 gold medals. The hero was the long-distance runner Hannes Kolehmainen, who won the 5000 m, 10 000 m and marathon and of whom it is said that he "ran Finland on to the map of the world". Between 1906 and 1994, Finland has won 137 Olympic gold medals, 35 of them in the Winter Olympics.

Athletics appear to be a Finnish strong point, especially long-distance running and javelin. The most famous Finnish runner was Paavo Nurmi who, in the Olympics between 1920 and 1928 won 9 gold and 3 silver medals. During his career he set 31 outdoor track world records. Almost in the same class was Nurmi's fellow runner Ville Ritola, who won five gold medals. The top runner in more recent times is

**Many feel that the 1952 Helsinki Olympics were the last true games.**

**The skiing couple Marja-Liisa and Harri Kirvesniemi have won many medals in winter olympics and world championships.**

Lasse Virén, who won the 5000 and 10 000 metre events in the 1972 and 1976 Olympics. In the javelin, Finns have three times walked off with triple victories.

In Olympic wrestling Finland was the leading country in the 1920s. It has also won medals in gymnastics, canoeing (gold medal by Mikko Kolehmainen in the 1992 Barcelona Olympic Games), javelin (silver medal by Seppo Räty in Barcelona) and many other events. The victories of oarsman Pertti Karppinen, chosen as Sportsman of the Year in 1979 and 1980, show that even such less traditional sports

have gained in popularity.

In cross-country skiing Finns have won many gold medals in the Olympics and world championships. The finest skiers of the older generation were the men Veli Saarinen, Veikko Hakulinen and Eero Mäntyranta, and the women Helena Takalo and Hilkka Riihivuori. Marja-Liisa Kirvesniemi became a national hero when she won three golds and one bronze at the Sarajevo Winter Olympics in 1984. A new star emerged at the 1988 Calgary Games, when engineering student Marjo Matikainen won a gold and two bronzes.

Ski-jumping is another event

**Teemu Selänne has scored a record number of goals for Winnipeg Jets at the NHL games.**

**Juha Kankkunen, world champion rally driver in 1986, 1987, 1991 and 1993.**

in which Finns shine. Matti Nykänen, Olympic winner and world master, dominated this event throughout the 1980s. At Calgary he became the first ski-jumper ever to win three golds in the same games. A ski-jump has been named after him in his home town of Jyväskylä. Ski-jumper Toni Nieminen won the 1992 World Cup and two gold medals and one bronze in the 1992 Winter Olympics in Albert-ville. He was the youngest winner ever in the history of the Winter olympics.

Ice hockey is so popular among youngsters that there is a special junior league. Many Finnish players, like Jari Kurri and Teemu Selänne have moved to the United States to play for professional teams.

The Finn Jari Litmanen who plays in Ajax, scored top goals in 1993/94 and was elecfed best football player in the Dutch league in that season.

Motor sports is another field in which Finns have become world famous. The best known rally drivers today are Marrku Alen, Ari Vatanen, Juha Kankkunen, Timo Salonen and Hannu Mikkola, winners of many world events. Pekka Vehkonen is the leading figure in motorcross racing, and Keke Rosberg was the first Formula One driver to come from Finland. He won the world championship in 1982 and, although he subsequently dropped out of racing, Keke is probably still the best-known Finnish sportsman in the world.

J. J. Lehto and Mika Häkkinen are current Formula-one drivers.

Although football is gaining in popularity, Finland is still streets away from becoming top of the European league. American football has also caught on, Finland even becoming European champions. It is probably true to say that there is a club in Finland for every conceivable sport.

## THE IMPORTANCE OF SPORT IN FINLAND

There are dozens of sports associations in Finland, the largest of which is SVUL (*Suomen Valtakunnan Urheilu-liitto*, the Finnish Central Sports Federation) with over 50 affiliated bodies and about 1.1 million individual members. The main centres for instruction and research are the universities of Jyväskylä and Tampere, the UKK Institute (named after President Kekkonen) in Tampere and a number of sports institutes. Sport receives financial support from the proceeds of the state-owned Oy Veikkaus Ab which runs football pools, trotting races, national and other lotteries.

Top athletes normally receive training grants from their own associations, and Olympic Games' entrants from the Finnish Olympic Committee. International competition winners are much feted heroes, often being given houses financed by donations or public subscription. As it is not possible to be a professional in Finland, many league-grade ice hockey and football players join European or American teams.

Finland's tremendous enthusiasm for sport is proven by its interest in hosting such major events as the 1952 Olympic Games and the first World Athletics Championships in 1983, both in Helsinki, as well as world ice hockey and skiing championships.

# THE FINNISH LIFESTYLE

Large families were quite normal in the old Finnish agrarian society, with several generations often living under the same roof. Even in the first half of this century it was still common that a son brought his bride home to live with his parents. As economic life diversified, more and more people changed over to the newer occupations and left to live in the towns and industrial centres. The large family disappeared, and nowadays it is very rare for grandparents to live with their children. The children have left to study or work elsewhere, leaving their parents to carry on in the home areas. When the time comes to go on pension, people often go to live in centres where they have acquired retirement flats, or to some senior citizen's centre especially designed to cater for their needs. There are also special homes for old people no longer capable of looking after themselves.

The mass migration of people from the countryside to the towns in the fifties and sixties caused an acute housing problem as it was almost impossible to find

**The nutritional value of Finnish rye bread is very high. In olden days, when the bread was baked at home, it was kept on rods suspended from the ceiling.**

rented accommodation because tenants were so protected in law that landlords had found more attractive ways of investing their wealth. These protective laws have now been repealed. People are, however, encouraged to buy their own homes, and it is nothing unusual for the first flat to be bought whilst still studying. Approximately 300 000 Finns own a summer cottage in addition to a flat or house. Even when students study in their home towns, they leave home to be free and independent.

Class distinctions in Finland have so narrowed that nowadays the difference is more in lifestyle than income. True poverty has virtually disappeared following the radical improvements in medical care, family allowances, unemployment benefits and pensions since the war. Although there are still income differences between occupations, basic necessities are guaranteed. There is now talk of the "new poor", people who live beyond their means and have sunk heavily into debt due to the availability of easy credit.

Differences between rural and urban lifestyles can be seen most clearly in consumption; what people spend their money on. In the larger cities the lifestyle is much the same as elsewhere in the world, and the effect of internationalisation on national culture is all too apparent. There are lesser opportunities for affluent living in the countryside.

Finns have a great respect for education, often considering it more important than income. Thus they respect the legal, medical and teaching professions, even though higher incomes could be earned elsewhere. For example, Finns rarely address each other as Mr or Mrs, but by professional titles such as Secretary or Director or academic qualifications such as Doctor or Professor.

With rapid industrialisation in the sixties, more and more women joined the labour force. Nowadays the majority of mothers of pre-school children go to work. Although the law requires that all under three-year-old children should have a place in the municipal day-care centres, this has not been possible to arrange yet. Most pre-school children spend 8 to 9 hours a day in some form of day care. The six-year-old children are in pre-school groups, and at seven they start school. Divorce, unfortunately, is on the increase, and some 15 % of all families are single-parent units. It is also increasingly normal to form common-law marriages, which have the same status in law as conventional marriages. The average Finnish family has two children, and only very few have four or more children. This is partly because ever more women spend longer studying or prefer to establish their careers before starting a family. It is nothing unusual for the first child to be born when the mother is over thirty. Few families, even rich ones, have domestics, so child upbringing and household chores are divided, often unevenly, between the parents.

Most Finns enjoy a month's holiday in summer and a week in winter, the latter normally taken during the school skiing holiday in February. Some spend their summers at summer cottages in the peaceful countryside, often beside a lake, others travelling around the country, camping or visiting relatives. An increasing number of people prefer to spend part of their holidays abroad, on the sunny beaches of Spain, Greece or Italy, or even travelling to the exotic East.

Sport is undoubtedly the most popular pastime in Finland: cross-country skiing, slalom or ice hockey in the winter, and swimming, walking, jogging, cycling, fishing, sailing or even

**Folk dancing is still very popular and courses well attended. The best time to see the dancers in their colourful national costumes is at Midsummer.**

playing golf in the summer. Finland has all the water and untouched nature that could be desired. Finns are also avid readers, borrowing an average of 17 books a year from their local libraries. These are very important leisure-time centres, especially in the countryside. Adult education is also very popular, with even the smallest village running courses in anything from information technology to Spanish. Watching television is also popular. There is a theatre in every town and a strong amateur theatrical movement in the countryside.

Because the Finnish language is so different from Indo-European languages, Finns are somewhat hesitant to exercise their linguistic skills in conversation with foreigners. They are often thought to be shy, but once you get to know them they are just the same as other people. There are perhaps some differences – the people from Savo and Karelia are considered more jovial and sociable than those from Häme and the southwest. Finns also have a tendency towards melancholy, which perhaps explains why dreamy tangoes are so popular in the restaurants where they go at the weekends to drink and dance. Drinking is also a problem for some, not that they drink too often, but too much at one time.

Although one cannot claim that Finns are religious, most of them are baptised and confirmed and prefer being married and buried by the church. Here, as elsewhere, the great Christian feasts of Christmas and Easter are very commercial, replete with traditional foods and the exchange of presents. These are old pagan customs which continue to thrive. The third great festival, Midsummer, is when the cities empty and the countryside is adorned with national costumes, flags and pennants. Mothers' Day is in May, Fathers' Day in November. Also every day is a nameday, celebrated in offices and homes with coffee

Finns are dead keen on sports and like to take part in mass events. The greatest of these is the Finlandia Skiing Race, when more than 10 000 people ski the 75 km from Hämeenlinna to Lahti.

**For most Finns the weekly sauna is still a must, and the best way to relax and forget about work.**

and cakes. As coffee is drunk on every possible social occasion, this has made Finns the world's largest coffee consumers. It is served on birthdays, namedays, engagement parties, reading the banns, weddings, funerals, graduations – the list is unending. And not just coffee, but a vast array of buns, cakes,

**Forests are an essential part of nature, somewhere to pick berries and mushrooms, or just breath fresh air and the resinous scent of the fir. The picture is of a typical birch glade.**

cookies and biscuits.

Whilst on the subject of these all-important Finnish rituals, one must not forget the sauna – and naturally the after-sauna coffee. In the countryside the whole family visits the sauna on Saturday evening, the sauna building normally ajoining the house or farm. In the towns apartment blocks have only one sauna for the tenants, so it is necessary to stagger visits throughout the week. The custom of visiting the sauna, however, has never been given up, and many newly built flats and houses in the towns now have their own sauna. Foreigners are always invited to have a sauna and beat out grime and tiredness with a fragrant bunch of leafy birch twigs. Finns are naturally proud that sauna is the one Finnish word that has spread throughout the world. The sauna is perhaps the oldest of all Finnish institutions. Its effect is not only cleansing, but relaxing and calming, and the feeling of well-being that comes with it is really worth experiencing. You can say no to almost anything else in Finland, but not to an invitation to a sauna. This is the only way in which a foreigner can ever get to grips with the true Finnish soul.

**Aalto, Jorma S.** (1935),
chancellor of Justice since 1986.
Doctor of Laws. Lecturer at the
universities of Helsinki and Turku since
1960, professor of procedural law since
1975. Parliamentary Ombudsman
1974–77, 1978–81 and 1982–86.

**Ahtisaari, Martti** (1937,)
president of the Republic, elementary
school teacher. Ambassador, eg. Dar es
Salaam 1937–77. Special representative
of the Secretary General of the United
Nations to Namibia 1973–77, Under-
Secretary of State for development
cooperation at the Ministry for Foreign
Affairs 1984–86. Assistant Under-
Secretary of the United Nations 1987–
91. Chairman of the United Nations
Bosnia-Herzegovina Working Group in
1992 and 1993. Secretary of State at the
Ministry for Foreign Affairs 1991–94.
Presi-dent of the Republic since 1994.

**Aho, Esko** (1954),
politician, Master of Political Science.
Member of Parliament since 1983.
Held various positions in the Centre
Party, chairman since 1990. Prime
minister since 1991.

**Berglund, Paavo** (1929),
conductor. First violinist of the Radio
Symphony Orchestra 1949–58,
conductor 1955–62, senior conductor
1962–71. Director of the Bournemouth
Symphony Orchestra 1972–79 and
Helsinki Philharmonic Orchestra
1975–79, visiting chief conductor of
the National Orchestra of Scotland
(Glasgow) since 1981, chief conductor
of the Stockholm Philharmonic Orchestra
since 1987. Special recognition for
interpretations of Sibelius, Brahms
and Shostakovitch.

**Bergman, Erik** (1911),
composer, professor, member of
the Academy of Finland. Studies in
Finland, Central Europe and Italy, music
critic, choir director and professor at
Sibelius Academy 1963–76. Leading
Finnish composer and pioneer of a new
music free of national traditions. Untiring
search for new paths and for an independent, unconventional approach.
Winner of the international Sibelius prize
in 1965.

**Cantell, Kari** (1932),
medical researcher, professor. Doctor of
Medicine and Surgery 1959, director of
the department of virology at the Institute of National Health. International
recognition for work on the use of
interferon in the treatment of cancer
and virus diseases.

**Donner, Jörn** (1933),
author, film producer and director,
member of Parliament. Book and cinema
critic for various Finnish and Swedish
papers. Managing director of the
Swedish Film Institute museum and
director of international operations, film
producer and company director in
1970s and 1980s. Directed over 40
films, many internationally recognised.
Well-known essayist and controversial
writer, whose extensive and diverse
output includes a series of novels about
the Finnish-Swedish upper class. Works
translated into several languages. First
winner of the prestigious Finlandia prize
for literature.

**Erkko, Aatos** (1932),
newspaper publisher. Editor-in-
chief of *Viikko-Sanomat* 1953–61
and *Helsingin Sanomat*, Finland's
largest national daily, 1961–72, and
managing director of their publishers
Sanoma Oy, 1965–76, and chairman
of the board since 1972.

**Gothoni , Ralf** (1946),
pianist, professor. Teacher at Sibelius
Academy 1968–69, 1970–73 and
professor 1991. Pianist with Royal Opera
of Stockholm 1969–70. Freelance
performer since 1973. Professor
Hamburg School of Music since 1987.
Lectures and courses in Finland and
abroad. Artistic director of Savonlinna
Opera Festival 1984–87, artistic director
of Finlandia Sinfonietta since 1989. Over
50 recordings, worked as conductor,
composed works for voice and piano.
Several awards and prizes, including the
internationally esteemed Gilmore Art
Award in 1994.

**Hägglund, Gustav** (1938),
commander-in-Chief of the Finnish
Defence Forces since 1994. Lieutenant-
general. Research professor at Harvard
University 1981–82. Commander of the
Finnish UN peacekeeping forces 1978–
79, commander of the UNDOF peacekeeping forces in Golan 1985–86 and
UNIFIL peacekeeping forces in South
Lebanon 1986–88. Commander of
the South-East Finland military area
1986–90. Chief of the General Head-
quarters 1990–94. Studies published
in Finland and the United States.

**Haavikko, Paavo** (1931),
author, publisher, honorary Doctor
of Philosophy and a member of the
Academy of Finland. One of the
foremost modern Finnish writers, first
Scandinavian to receive the coveted
Neustadt prize for literature in 1984.
Nine state prizes for literature. Has
written poetry, aphorisms, radio and
theatre plays, librettos, short stories,
novels and essays. Poetry translated
into many languages. Wrote the script
for the TV film *The Age of Iron*, which
won the Prix Italia in 1983. Member
of the board of the Finnish Society of
Authors since the early 1960s. Literary
director of Otava Publishing Company
1967–83, managing director of Arthouse
Publishing Company 1985.

**Hämäläinen, Sirkka** (1939),
governor of the Bank of Finland, D.Sc.
(Econ.). Various positions in the Bank
of Finland, acting head of economics
department 1961–81, director 1982–91,
member of the board 1991–92, governor
since 1992. Also director general, economics department of the Ministry of
Finance 1982–91.

**Harlin, Renny** (1959),
movie producer and director. Short film producer and director for advertizing bureaus and Finnish Broadcasting Company 1979–82. Productions and directions in Hollywood since 1983 include Arctic Heat, Prison Nightmare on Elm Street 4, Ford Fairlane, Die Hard 2, Rambling Rose and Cliffhanger. Awards for advertising and short films in Finland, international film festivals and two-time Oscar candidate.

**Hiltunen, Eila** (1922),
sculptress, professor. Numerous exhibitions abroad, including New York 1969 and Rome 1985, and others supported by Ministry for Foreign Affairs in Ottawa and Philadelphia in 1982. Works in several museums in Finland and abroad. Most famous work is the Sibelius Monument (1967) in Helsinki, studies for which are in Montreal and outside the UN building in New York. Eila Hiltunen's sculptures are usually large and impressive.

**Herlin, Pekka** (1932),
board chairman, B. Sc. (Econ.). Career at Kone Corporation, administrative director 1958–62, deputy managing director 1962–64, managing director 1964–87, chairman of the board since 1987. Kone Corporation, which has subsidiaries and factories in some 15 countries, produces mainly lifts.

**Holmberg, Kaarle (Kalle)** (1939),
theatre director. Received widespread recognition for opera directions. Most known abroad for his direction of *The Red Line* at the Metropolitan in 1983. Other successes include winning the Prix Italia in 1983 for *The Age of Iron*. Served as manager of the Helsinki Student Theatre, director of Helsinki and Turku city theatres, and YLE radio and TV theatres, principal of the Finnish Academy of Dramatic Art, teacher at the Sibelius Academy, manager of KOM Theatre 1981–82, senior director of the Helsinki City Theatre 1984–93.

**Hynninen, Jorma** (1941),
opera singer. School teacher 1964,
studied music in Finland and abroad in
late 1950s and early 1970s, won
Lappeenranta song competition 1969,
soloist at the Finnish National Opera
since 1970, and artistic director 1984–
90. Artistic director of the Savonlinna
Opera Festival 1991–. Performed in
operas and lied concerts in all major
music centres. One of the leading
baritones of our time. Leading opera
roles include the Count of Almaviva in
the *Marriage of Figaro*, Figaro in the
*Barber of Seville*, Rodrigo in *Don Carlos*,
and Topi in *The Red Line*.

**Ihamuotila, Jaakko** (1939),
CEO, engineer. Assistant and later
assistant professor in physics at the
Helsinki University of Technology
in 1960s, planning engineer with Imatran
Voima Oy 1966–68, planning engineer,
assistant director, planning director,
managing director and vice chairman of
the board of Valmet Oy 1968–79, CEO
and chairman of the board of Neste Oy
since 1980. Member of the boards of
many companies and business
organisations.

**Ihalainen, Lauri** (1947),
chairman of the Central Organisation of
Finnish Trade Unions (SAK) since 1990.
Previously occupied various positions in
SAK, including youth secretary 1970–77,
organisation secretary 1977–84, secretary 1984–90.

**Jakobson, Max** (1923),
managing director, diplomat, honorary
Doctor of Political Science (Helsinki).
Director for political affairs at the Ministry
for Foreign Affairs in 1960s, Finland's
permanent representative to the UN
1965–72, Finnish ambassador to Stockholm 1972–74, managing director of the
Council of Economic Organisations of
Finland (EVA) 1975–84. Published
several works on recent Finnish history
which have been translated into different
languages.

**Jansson, Tove** (1914),
authoress, artist, honorary Doctor
of Philosophy (Åbo Academy).
Art studies in Finland and abroad.
Prizes in Finland and other countries.
First book, *Moomin and the Comet*,
published 1946. Since then tens of
Moomin books have delighted children
throughout the world. Translations into
almost 30 languages. Several literary
prizes, including H. C. Andersen medal,
Austrian state prize, Swedish Academy
prize, and Le Prix de l'Office Chrétien
du Livre.

**Kahri, Tapani** (1938),
managing director of the Finnish
Employers' Federation (STK) since 1988,
Master of Laws. Various positions in
STK since 1965, director 1971–79,
managing director of the Finnish
Employers' General Group 1980–88,
managing director of STK since 1988.

**Johannes**
(Rinne, Johannes Wilho) (1923),
archbishop of the Finnish Orthodox
Church (Finland's second official
church), Doctor of Theology. Assistant
bishop 1969, bishop of Helsinki 1970,
metropolitan of Helsinki 1972,
archbishop since 1987.

**Kamu, Okko** (1946),
conductor. Studied the violin and
played in several orchestras. Won the
international Karajan competition for
young conductors, Berlin, 1969. Has
served as senior conductor of the Radio
Symphony Orchestra 1972–77, Oslo
Philharmonic Orchestra 1975–79, artistic
director of the Helsinki Philharmonic
Orchestra 1981–88. Several times
visiting conductor abroad. Known for his
great musical sensitivity and vitality,
which comes into its own in a classical-
romantic repertoire.

**Kankkunen, Juha** (1959),
rally car driver. World rally car champion
1986, 1987, 1991 and 1993, silver
medal 1992 and bronze medal 1989
and 1990. Chosen Sportsman of the
year in Finland in 1993.

**Koivisto, Mauno** (1923),
President of the Republic 1982–94,
Doctor of Philosophy. Served in various
positions in banking since 1957,
chairman of the board of the Bank of
Finland 1968–82. Minister of Finance in
several governments, prime minister
1968–70 and 1979–82, represents the
Social Democratic Party. Assumed the
duties of president when President
Kekkonen fell sick in autumn 1981,
elected president in 1982 and again
in 1988.

**Kaurismäki, Mika** (1955),
film producer and director. With his
brother **Aki** (1957) represents the
younger generation in the Finnish
film industry. They have produced and
directed films together and separately,
in Finland and abroad, and which have
achieved international success.

**Kokkonen, Joonas** (1921),
composer, member of the Academy
of Finland. Teacher at the Sibelius
Academy in the 1940s and 1950s,
and professor of composition 1959–63,
after which he was appointed to the
Academy of Finland. Successful
composer of operas and chamber
music, and as a sym-phonist has made
a highly original contribution to Finnish
music. Won the international Sibelius
prize in 1973. Main opera, *The Last
Temptations*, has been performed at
the New York Metropolitan.

**Kukkasjärvi, Irma** (1941),
textile designer. Designer with Arola Oy
1973–76, own studio 1968–73
and again since 1976. Teacher at
the University of Industrial Art since
1977, Finnish member of World Crafts
Council 1973–75, occupies many
positions in Finnish art associations.
Participated in exhibitions in Europe,
Japan, Australia and the United States.
Awarded numerous prizes, including
Textile Artist of the Year in 1984. One of
the foremost textile designers in Finland,
admired for her huge, sculptured ryijy
rugs. Has been much influenced by
Japanese textile design.

**Liikanen, Erkki** (1950),
EU comissioner, politician, M.Sc.(Pol.).
Member of Parliament 1972–90.
Secretary of the Social Democratic Party
1981–87, Minister of Finance 1987–90.
Ambassador of Finland to the European
Community and later the European
Union 1990–94. EU comissioner since
1995.

**Leiviskä, Juha** (1936)
Architect, artist professor. Own
architectural office 1967–77, in part-
nership with Vilhelm Helander since
1976. Major works include Kouvola
town hall (with Bertel Saarnio) 1964–68,
Myyrmäki church and parish centre
1980–84, German Embassy in Helsinki
(with Rosemarie Schnitzler–Mattila and
Nicholas Mayow), Hakushi restaurant
design, Japan and Smista Business
Centre, Huddinge, Sweden 1990–91.
Several first prizes in architectural
competitions, numerous other prizes
and stipends, member of architectural
competition juries. Works often featured
in domestic and foreign professinal
journals.

**Lindfors, Stefan** (1962),
interior architect, furniture designer.
Teacher at the University of Industrial
Art, Helsinki University of Technology,
Danish Design School and Oslo Univer-
sity of Industrial Art, professor at the
Kansas City Art Institute since 1993.
Stage settings, designs for lamps,
furniture, store interiors, exhibitions,
catalogues, advertising campaigns and
packagings for Finnish and foreign
companies. Sculptures in eg. Helsinki
airport domestic terminal, works in
Finnish museums and in Gothenburg.
STO Interior Design Award 1993, Georg
Jensen Prize 1992, Väinö Tanner
Trailblazer Award 1992 and Finnish
Foundation of Visual Arts Stipend 1992.

**Lipponen, Paavo** (1941),
chairman Finnish Social Democratic
Party. B.Sc. (Econ.). Occupied several
positions in the party since 1967.
Member of Parliament 1983–87 and
since 1991–. Political secretary to Prime
Minister 1979–82. City of Helsinki
councillor since 1993. Member of the
board of several companies and
societies.

**Mattila, Karita** (1960),
opera soprano. Won the Lappeenranta
(1981) and BBC Cardiff (1983) voice
competitions. Successful performances
in the Finnish National Opera and with
opera companies in Paris, London and
Brussels, mainly singing Mozart operas.

**Matomäki, Tauno** (1937),
CEO, M. Sc. (Engineering). Director of
offshore industry in Rauma-Repola Oy,
deputy managing director 1983–86,
CEO since 1987. Company (renamed
Repola Oy in 1991) is one of the largest
private corporations in Finland.

**Norrback, Ole** (1941),
politician, teacher. Member of
Parliament since 1979, Minister of
Defense 1987–90, Minister of Education
1990–91, Minister of Transportation
since 1991. Chairman of the Swedish
People's Party since 1990.

**Ollila, Jorma** (1950)
CEO, M.Sc. (Econ.), M.Sc. (Eng.), M.Sc. (Pol.). Various positions in Oy Nokia Ab, deputy managing director international operations 1985-86, deputy managing director for finance 1986-89, managing director Nokia Mobile Phones 1990-92, since 1992 group CEO and chairman of the board. On the boards of several Finnish and foreign companies and business organisations.

**Pallasmaa, Juhani** (1936),
architect, professor. Joint architectural design work with various Finnish architects since 1962, own architectural office since 1983. Professor of Architecture Helsinki University of Technology since 1991, director of the Museum of Finnish Archi-tecture 1976–83, rector University of Industrial Art 1972–74. Major works include Finnish Institute in Paris 1991, Helsinki East Centre shopping mall 1992. Has designed town planning, industrial art and art exhibitions. Visiting professor of architecture at foreign universities, editor of books and exhibition catalogues, lectures and articles. Honorary member of the International Academy of Architecture and Institute of American Architects.

**Potila, Antti** (1938),
company president, M. Sc. (Comm.). Various positions in Oy Strömberg Ab 1964–78, managing director 1979–83, CEO of Rauma-Repola Oy 1984–87, president of Finnair Oy since 1987. Served on the boards of several companies.

**Pöyry, Jaakko** (1924),
M. Sc. (Engineering), professor. Various planning and managerial positions in Oy Wärtsilä Ab 1947–56, managing director of Murto and Pöyry Engineering Office 1958–61, managing director of Jaakko Pöyry Engineering Office 1961–77, chairman of the board of Jaakko Pöyry Group since 1977. The Jaakko Pöyry Group operates forest industry planning and project services, research projects, and has offices in different parts of the world.

**Rehn, Elisabeth** (1935),
minister of Defence. B.Sc. (Econ.).
Active in business life and education.
Member of Parliament 1979–. Chairman
of the Parliamentary Group of the
Swedish People's Party 1987–90.
Minister of Defence since 1990.
Candidate in the 1994 Presidential
elections. Member of the boards of
several foundations and companies.

**Sallinen, Aulis** (1935),
composer. Manager of the Radio
Symphony Orchestra 1960–70, teacher
at the Sibelius Academy 1965–76, artist
professor since 1976. Sallinen's style
has a polymorphic and original expression. He has composed symphonies, a
cello concerto and music for children's
choirs. His *The Horseman*, *The Red Line*
and *The King Goes Forth to France*
played a vital role in the rebirth of
Finnish opera.

**Saariaho, Kaija** (1952),
composer. Studied composition in
Germany. She worked in several
electronic music studios, at present
in IRCAM, the Institute of Acoustic Music
at the Pompidou Centre, Paris.
International awards include Prix
Italia in radio programme series 1988,
Goldene Nica prize at Ars Electronica
festival, Linz, Austria, 1989.

**Salolainen, Pertti** (1940),
politician, M. Sc. (Econ). Post graduate
studies in London, worked for the BBC.
Worked for YLE during 1960s as a
news reporter and producer of economic programmes, and as London
correspondent 1966–69. Department
manager of the Finnish Employers'
Confederation since 1969. Member of
Parliament since 1970. Chairman of the
National Coalition Party 1991–94. Chief
negotiator with the European Union, first
chairman of the economic committee of
Inter-Parliamentary Union and member
of the legal committee of the Nordic
Council. Minister of Foreign Trade
since 1987.

**Salonen, Esa-Pekka** (1958), conductor, composer. Studied composition and conducting in both Finland and Italy. International breakthrough after conducting Mahler's Third Symphony in London in 1983. Chief conductor of the Swedish Radio Symphony Orchestra since 1985, visiting conductor of the London Philharmonic Orchestra 1985–88, regular visits to Oslo, also to Los Angeles where he has been chief conductor since 1992.

**Sarmanto, Heikki** (1939), composer, pianist. Has composed a jazz mass and lied-type songs. Successfully combines elements of jazz and concert music. Several Finnish and international awards, including first prize in piano and orchestra series at Montreux 1971.

**Saraste, Jukka** (1956), conductor. Visiting conductor with several orchestras in Finland and abroad, including Finnish Radio Symphony Orchestra 1985–87. Chief conductor of Scottish Chamber Orchestra since 1986. Chief conductor of Radio Symphony Orchestra since 1987. Conductor of Toronto Symphony Orchestra since 1994.

**Sarpaneva, Timo** (1926), artistic director, professor. Graduated from School of Applied Arts 1948. Worked as designer and artistic director in several companies. Designed art glass and objects in glass, porcelain, steel and cast iron, as well as clothes. Numerous exhibitions in Finland and abroad, works in many museums. Among important international awards are the Lunning Prize and the Italian president's gold medal. Honorary doctorate from Royal College of Arts.

**Sundberg, Matti** (1942)
CEO, M. Sc. (Econ.). Occupied several positions of responsibility in industry, among them managing director of Metsä-Botnia 1976-86 and Ovako 1986-91. Since 1991 CEO of Valmet, a major Finnish high-tech multinational specialising in machine engineering.

**Uosukainen, Riitta** (1942)
Speaker of the Finnish Parliament. M.A. (Phil.). Worked in publishing and as a Finnish language teacher in schools and universities. Member of Parliament since 1983. Minister of Education 1991–94, speaker of the Finnish Parliament since 1994. On the boards of several cultural organisations and companies. Author of a Finnish grammar.

**Toikka, Oiva** (1931),
industrial designer. Teacher at the School of Applied Arts 1960–63, designer at Wärtsilä's Arabia factory and Nuutajärvi Glass. Glass works include utility designs, art and unique pieces, as well as sculptures. He has exhibited abroad and has works displayed in many foreign museums. Awards include the coveted Lunning Prize 1970, Asahi Shimbun and Hokkaido Museum of Modern Art World Glass Now prize 1985.

**Uotinen, Jorma** (1950)
Internationally recognised ballet dancer and choreographer. Dancer with Finnish National Opera 1970–76, member of Group de Recherches Théâtrales de l´Opera de Paris. Dancing master with City of Helsinki Theatre 1982–91, member of the board and director of the dance group 1987–91. Director Finnish National Ballet since 1992. Choreographs include Trio, The Endless Enigma, The Forgotten Horizon, Unisono, Pierrot Lunaire, Kalevala, Ballet Pathetique, The Dance Floor on the Mountain and Cable, often in collaboration with Pirjo and Matti Bergström or Carolyn Carson. Choreography for the Finnish versions of the musicals Chicago and Cats.

**Vainio, Vesa** (1942)
CEO, Master of Laws. Occupied executive positions in many companies, most recently deputy managing director of the wood and paper company Kymmene Oy 1985-91 and its managing director 1991-92. Member of the board of many Finnish companies. Managing director of the Union Bank of Finland 1992-93 and its CEO since 1993.

**Vikström, John** (1931),
archbishop of the Evangelical Lutheran Church of Finland, Doctor of Theology. Teacher and reader at Åbo Academy in 1960s, assistant professor 1970. Occupied many administrative positions in the church in the 1970s, bishop of the diocese of Porvoo 1970–82, archbishop since 1982. Member of the central committee of the World Council of Churches since 1983. Published numerous works on religious subjects.

**Wessberg, Arne** (1943)
Director General of the Finnish Broadcasting Company. Various positions in advertising 1966–71. Reporter on economic affairs with Channel 2 1971–75, Programme director for Channel 1 1975–76, Personnel director STS Bank 1976–79, Director Channel 1 1980–89, Director Channel 2 1990–94. Director General of the Finnish Broadcasting Company since 1994. Occupies positions of trust in several Finnish and international radio, TV and cultural organisations.

**Voutilainen, Pertti** (1940)
CEO, M.Sc. (Eng.), M.Sc. (Econ.). Various positions in the mining and metal company Outokumpu Oy since 1964, managing director and chairman of the board 1983-91. Member of the board of many Finnish companies. Since 1992 chairman of the board and CEO of the Kansallis-Osake-Pankki bank.

# SELECTED BIBLIOGRAPHY

## General Works

Facts about Finland, Helsinki, Otava, 1991.

Find out about Finland, Helsinki, Otava, 1991.

Focus on Finland, Helsinki, Foreign Office Publications, 1990.

Kuusi, Pekka, This World of Man, Oxford, Pergamon Press, 1985.

Vatanen, Ari & Väisänen, Vesa, Every Second Counts, SAF Publishing, London 1988.

Visions of Finland, Helsinki, Kirja-yhtymä, 1988.

Welcome to Finland. Bienvenue en Finlande. Willkommen in Finnland. 29th edition, Welscan Ag International Publishers, Denmark, 1989.

## Geography and Travels

Arstila, A., The Finnish Sauna, Espoo, Weilin & Göös, 1983.

The Face of Finland, Helsinki, Otava, 1983.

Finland. Land of the Midnight Sun. Land der Mitternachtsonne, Helsinki Valitut Palat/Readers' Digest, 1980.

Finland Handbook 1991, Helsinki, The Finnish Tourist Board and the Government Printing Centre, 1991.

Fodor's Stockholm, Copenhagen, Oslo, Helsinki, Reykjavik, London, Hodder & Stoughton, 1983.

Hautala, Hannu, Winter on the Finnish Taiga, Helsinki, Otava, 1990.

Huovinen, Veikko & Kemilä, Eero, Seitsemän sinisen takana – Kuvakirja Sotkamosta. Bortom sju blånande berg – Bilder från Sotkamo. Behind Seven Blue-Tinged Hills – Sotkamo in Pictures. Und lau schimmern die Berge – Bilder aus Sotkamo, Helsinki, Otava, 1986.

Häyrinen, Urpo, Lapinmaa. Lapland. Helsinki, Kirjayhtymä, 1975.

Jäppinen, Jussi & Mäkelä, Pekka, Keski-Suomi lähikuvassa. Mellersta Finland i närbild. A Portrait of Central Finland. Mittel-Finnland in Nahaufname, Helsinki, Otava, 1989.

Kallio, Veikko, Finland Cultural Perspectives, Helsinki, WSOY, 1989.

Kautia, Lauri & Seppälä, Raimo, Tampere keväästä kevääseen/från vår till vår/From spring to spring/ rund ums Jahr, Helsinki, Otava, 1983. Lappi väreissä. Lapland in Colours, Helsinki, Tammi, 1983.

Mead, W.R., A Historical Geography of Scandinavia, London, Academic Press, 1981.

Pitkänen, Matti A., Lapin värit, ruska ja kaamos. The Colours of Lapland, Helsinki, Otava, 1983.

Pitkänen, Matti A. & Pitkänen, Ilkka, Poromiehet. The Lapps and their Reindeer, Espoo, Weilin & Göös, 1984.

Suomen Gastronomien Seura. Gastronomic Society of Finland. Syö hyvin Helsingissä. Where to Eat in Helsinki, Jyväskylä, Tietoteos, 1990.

Tanttu, Anna-Maija & Tanttu, Juha, Food from Finland. A Finnish Cookbook, Helsinki, Otava, 1988.

Valon maa. Land of Light. Suomen luonto kuvina. Northern Pictures, Helsinki, Kirjayhtymä, 1983.

Welin, P.-O. & Othman, Hans, Museoiden Turku. Museernas Åbo. Turku, City of Museums. Museen-stadt Turku, Helsinki, Otava, 1989.

Welin, P.-O. & Othman, Hans, Turku. Åbo. The City of Turku. Die Stadt Turku, Helsinki, Otava, 1990.

## History and Politics

Alapuro, Risto, State and Revolution in Finland, Berkley, The University of California Press, 1990.

Jakobson, Max, Finland: Myth and

Reality, Helsinki, Otava, 1987.

JUTIKKALA, EINO & PIRINEN, KAUKO, A History of Finland, London, New York, Praeger, 1974.

JÄGERSKIÖLD, STIG, Mannerheim. Marshal of Finland, London, Hurst & Company, 1986.

KIRBY, D.G., Finland and Russia 1808–1920: from Autonomy to Independence, London, Macmillan, 1975.

KIRBY, D.G., Finland in the Twentieth Century. A History and an Interpretation, London, Hurst & Co., 1979.

KLINGE, MATTI, Brief History of Finland, Helsinki, Otava, 1991.

KLINGE, MATTI, Let Us Be Finns, Helsinki, Otava, 1991.

KOIVISTO, MAUNO, Landmarks, Helsinki, Kirjayhtymä, 1985.

KORHONEN, KEIJO, Urho Kekkonen – A Statesman for Peace, Helsinki, Otava, 1975.

PAASIVIRTA, JUHANI, Finland and Europe. The Period of Autonomy & International Crises in 1808–1914, University of Minnesota Press, 1982.

PAASIVIRTA, JUHANI, Finland and Europe. The Early Years of Independence 1917–1939, Helsinki, Societas Historica Finlandiae,1989.

POLVINEN, TUOMO, Between East and West. Finland in International Politics, 1944–47, Minneapolis, University of Minneapolis Press, 1986.

PUNTILA, L.A., The Political History of Finland 1809–1966, Helsinki, Otava, 1975.

RAUTKALLIO, HANNU, Finland and the Holocaust. The Rescue of Finland's Jews, New York, Holocaust Library, 1988.

The United States and Finland: An Enduring Relationship 1919–1989. Yhdysvaltain ja Suomen suhteiden kehitys, Helsinki, The United States Information Service, 1989.

UPTON, ANTHONY F., Finland, Nineteen Thirty Nine to Nineteen Forty, University of Delaware Press, 1979.

UPTON, ANTHONY F., The Finnish Revolution, University of Minnesota Press, 1980.

## Finnish Language and Dictionnaries

AALTIO, MAIJA-HELLIKKI, Finnish for Foreigners. Helsinki, Otava, 1990.

ALANNE, V.S., Suomalais-englantilainen suursanakirja. Finnish-English General Dictionary, Helsinki, WSOY, 1984.

ATKINSON, JOHN, A Finnish Grammar, Helsinki, The Finnish Literature Society, 1981.

HURME, RAIJA, PESONEN, MARITTA & SYVÄOJA, OLLI, Englantilais-suomalainen suursanakirja. English-Finnish General Dictionary, Helsinki, WSOY, 1990.

RIIKONEN, EEVA & TUOMIKOSKI, AUNE, Englantilais-suomalainen sanakirja. English-Finnish Dictionary, Helsinki, Otava, 1979.

TAKALA, SAULI, Suomi-englanti-suomi. Kasvatus- ja opetusalan sanasto. Finnish-English-Finnish. A Vocabulary of Educational and Pedagogical Terms, Helsinki, Otava, 19

## Art and Architecture

Ateneum Guide. From Isak Wacklin to Wäinö Aaltonen, Helsinki, The Fine Arts Academy of Finland and Otava, 1987.

BOULTON SMITH J., The Golden Age of Finnish Art, Helsinki, Otava, 1980.

Finnish Vision: Modern Art, Architecture and Design, Helsinki, Otava, 1983.

HAUSEN, MARIKA, MIKKOLA, KIRMO, AMBERG, ANNA-LIISA, AND VALTO, TYTTI, Hvitträsk. The Home as a Work of Art, Helsinki, Otava, 1988.

HAUSEN, MARIKA, MIKKOLA, KIRMO, AMBERG, ANNA-LIISA, AND VALTO, TYTTI, Eliel Saarinen. Projects 1896–1923, Helsinki, Otava, 1990.

Heijastuksia Suomesta. Finnish Reflections. Space. Time. Objects.

Helsinki, Kirjayhtymä, 1981.

KALIN, KAJ, Sarpaneva, Helsinki, Otava, 1986.

QUANTRILL, MALCOLM, Alvar Aalto. A Critical Study, Helsinki, Otava, 1983.

SCHILDT, GÖRAN, Alvar Aalto. The Decisive Years, Helsinki, Otava, 1986.

VALKONEN, MARKKU. Finnish Art over the Centuries, Helsinki, Otava, 1992.

TAPIO WIRKKALA. Helsinki, the Finnish Socienty of Arts and Crafts, 1981.

BJÖRN WECKSTRÖM, Helsinki, Otava, 1980.

## Music and Literature

CARPELAN, BO, Axel, London, Carcanet, 1989.

Finnish Short Stories, St. Paul, Minnesota, 1982.

HAAVIKKO, PAAVO, Selected Poems, London, Penguin, 1974.

JANSSON, TOVE, Sun City, London, Hutchinson, 1977.

The Kalevala. Epic of the Finnish People, Helsinki, Otava, 1990.

KIHLMAN, CHRISTER, The Blue Mother, Lincoln, Nebraska University Press, 1990.

KILPI, EEVA, Tamara, New York, Delacorte Press, 1978.

KIVI, ALEKSIS, Seven Brothers, Helsinki, Tammi, 1973.

KUNNAS, MAURI, Santa Claus, London, Methuen, 1982.

KURTEN, BJÖRN, Dance of the Tiger, London, Abacus, 1982.

LEINO, EINO, Whitsongs, London, The Menard Press, 1978.

LINNA; VÄINÖ, The Unknown Soldier, Helsinki, WSOY, 1975.

MERI, VEIJO, The Manila Rope, New York, Knopf, 1967.

OLSSON, HAGAR, The Woodcarver and Death, Madison and Milwaukee, 1965.

PAULAHARJU, SAMULI, Arctic Twilight. Old Finnish tales, Portland, Oregon, American Literary Heritage Foundation, 1982.

PEKKANEN, TOIVO, My Childhood, Madison, University of Wisconsin Press, 1966.

SAARIKOSKI, PENTTI, Poems 1958–1980, West Branch, Iowa, The Toothpaste Press, 1983.

SILLANPÄÄ, FRANS EMIL, Meek Heritage, New York, 1973.

SÖDERGRAHN, EDITH, Comlete Poems, Newcastle-upon-Tyne, Bloodaxe Books Ltd., 1984.

TAWASTSTJERNA, ERIK, Sibelius, volume I, London, Faber & Faber, 1976.

TIKKANEN, HENRIK, A Winter's Day, New York, Pantheon books, 1980.

TIKKANEN, MÄRTA, Manrape, London, Virago, 1978.

WALTARI, MIKA, Sinuhe, the Egyptian, Bath, Chivers, 1973.

**Illustrations:**

Defence forces archives p. 176, 179; Dentaldepot p. 90; Disabled War Veterans' Association of Finland p. 87; El Rod Oy Opa p. 136; Finland's Soprtmuseum Foundation p. 159; Finnair p. 183; Finnish Broadcasting Corporation p. 182; Oy Fiskars Ab p. 75; Fotoni p. 23; Hannu Hautala p. 9 (below); Helo Oy p. 171; Helsinki University of Technology p. 108; Harri Hietala p. 102; Seppo Hilpo p. 147 (below); Urpo Häyrinen pp. 21, 30, 33; Iittala-Nuutajärvi Oy p. 134 (below); Tove Jansson p. 123; Juha Kalliolahti p. 13; Seppo Keränen p. 10 (above); Juhani Kohonen p. 115; Kone oy p. 175; Lehtikuva pp. 36–37, 54, 58, 65 (above), 81, 96–97, 107, 124–125, 129, 130–131, 133, 140 (above), 160–161, 162 (both), 168–169, 173 (Ahtisaari, Aho), 178 (Johannes), 179 (Aki and Mika Kaurismäki), 180 (Liikanen), 181 (Mattila, Matomäki), 182 (Norrback), 183 (Saariaho), 184 (Sarmanto), 186 (Tarjanne), 187 (Toikka, Wahlroos): Leipätiedotus p. 164; Pekka Lempiäinen p. 22, 99, 104, 166–167; Anneke Lipsanen p. 114; Luonnonkuva-arkisto p.89; Luhta Oy p. 77; Museum of Finnish Architecture pp. 140–141 (below), 145; Museum of Finnish Industrial Design pp. 116, 134; Lauri Mäkinen pp. 4, 12, 52, 83, 100; Juha Mälkönen p. 9 (above); Nasakuva p. 175; Oy Nautor Ab p. 70–71; Oy Nokia Ab pp. 75, 188; Paavo Ojasti p. 5; Otava pp. 46, 53, 173, 174, 175, 176, 177, 178, 179, 180, 181, 182, 184, 185, 186, 187, 188; Pressfoto pp. 18 (below), 48, 64–65, 80, 105; Martti Rantanen p. 72 (above); Rauma-Repola Offshore Oy p. 69; Rautakirja Oy pp. 154–155; Arno Rautavaara pp. 10–11 (below); Tapani Romppainen p. 95; Matti Ruotsalainen pp. 31, 46, 50, 127, 128, 146; Ritva Räty p. 170; SAK p. 172; P. Sarvas p. 42; Sky-Foto pp. 7 (both), 92–93; Studio Pitkänen Ky p. 40; STK p. 178; Heikki Suni p. 62; Suomen selkäinsti-tuutti p. 85; Vaisala Oy p. 74; Valio p. 24 (both); Valmet Oy p. 71; Matti Valta pp. 16–17; Rafael Wardi p. 147 (above); P.-O. Welin pp. 26–27, 28, 29, 35, 44–45; Viking Line p. 18 (above); Yhtyneet Kuvalehdet pp. 14–15, 56, 60–61, 138–139, 143, 148–149, 151, 153, Yhtyneet paperitehtaat p. 72–73.